BRIDE OF DARK AND STORMY

Yet More of
the Best (?)
from the
Bulwer-Lytton
Fiction Contest

Compiled by

SCOTT RICE

Penguin Books

PENGUIN BOOKS
Published by the Penguin Group
Viking Penguin Inc., 40 West 23rd Street,
New York, New York 10010, U.S.A.
Penguin Books Ltd, 27 Wrights Lane,
London W8 5TZ, England
Penguin Books Australia Ltd, Ringwood,
Victoria, Australia
Penguin Books Canada Ltd, 2801 John Street,
Markham, Ontario, Canada L3R 1B4
Penguin Books (N.Z.) Ltd, 182–190 Wairau Road,
Auckland 10, New Zealand

Penguin Books Ltd, Registered Offices:
Harmondsworth, Middlesex, England

First published in Penguin Books 1988
Published simultaneously in Canada

LIBRARY OF CONGRESS CATALOGING IN PUBLICATION DATA
Bride of dark and stormy : yet more of the best (?) from the Bulwer
-Lytton Fiction Contest / compiled by Scott Rice.
p.   cm.
ISBN 0 14 01.0304 X
1. Authorship—Anecdotes, facetiae, satire, etc.   2. Openings
(Rhetoric)—Anecdotes, facetiae, satire, etc.   3. Fiction—
Technique—Anecdotes, facetiae, satire, etc.   I. Rice, Scott.
PN6231.A77B7   1988
818'.5402'08—dc19   87-28967
                                                          CIP

Printed in the United States of America by
R. R. Donnelley & Sons Company, Harrisonburg, Virginia
Set in Caslon 540
Designed by Beth Tondreau Design

CONTENTS

INTRODUCTION

The Bulwer-Lytton Fiction Contest is an annual competition sponsored by San Jose State University which challenges entrants to compose the opening sentence to the worst of all possible novels. The contest takes its name from Edward George Bulwer-Lytton, an industrious Victorian novelist whose *Paul Clifford* (1830) set a standard for pot-boiling openers: "It was a dark and stormy night . . ." The following is the third collection of contest entries published by Penguin Books.

The goal of the Bulwer-Lytton Fiction Contest, aside from promoting truth, justice, and The American Way, is to provide a forum for unappreciated talent. In other words, the BLFC is looking for people who want to be famous authors.

Besides simply providing an outlet for fresh talent, the sponsors of the BLFC believe that it is time to supply some practical assistance to those who have not yet been able to crack the best-seller lists and thereby reap obscene profits from the publishing industry. Many insidious forces conspire to frustrate aspiring writers, but we believe that the principal culprit is the state of writing instruction itself. The lamentable fact is that bookstores are glutted with texts offering advice to writers, most of it impractical and some even deliberately wrong-headed. What follows is thus a generous attempt to rectify this situation and provide a succinct statement of all that you will ever need to know about writing.

There has been a lot of foolishness written about writing, most of it by writers (which is just about what you could expect). Writers are seldom more creative than when inventing stories about the mystery and the difficulty of writing. Professional writers, the ones making megabucks with their ballpoints and word processors, habitually exaggerate the effort that goes into writing. It is something they do to stifle competition and keep a good thing all for themselves.

We cannot blame professional writers for wanting to keep the good life all to themselves, but you aspiring writers know full well what it is like to be authors: the French restaurants, the talk shows, the autograph hounds and groupies, seeing your books in supermarkets and airports and bus depots, interviewing the actors and actresses who want to portray your characters in big-budget movies, consulting with the producers who will scrupulously insist on preserving every detail of your stories, posing for dust-jackets with pipe or Afghan hound, and, of course, the flattery of reviewers and the servility of editors.

The purpose of this book is to explode all the myths that are calculated to frighten away beginners and that gull the naïve into busting their tails to do the impossible, or at least the difficult (years of saturation in a subject, endless rewrites, etc.). Don't allow yourself to be dissuaded, or even discouraged. Experienced professionals are simply people who have mastered some basic tricks of the trade, little, easy-to-grasp tips that can skyrocket you (*you*, not the pretender down the street) into authorly success. It can be you on the *Tonight Show*, you married to a movie star, you worrying about how to invest your royalty checks.

Professional writers look with scorn on self-help books such as this one, and for good reason: they are afraid someone will inadvertently let slip some trade secrets. But this book is not like others of its kind. Most of them offer only technique and method; this one offers you secrets and magic. That is right.

This book is about the shortcuts that will enable you to crank out book after book, novel after novel. However, we don't mean to suggest that there is an easy formula for instant success. The term *formula* makes the process sound too complicated.

The first thing to know, then, is that writing is not really work (though you will learn to describe it as such once you are famous). It is really a game. Only no-talent types have to apply themselves very hard. If you find yourself struggling on a draft, it is because you are doing it wrong, because you have not learned to access your creative juices. When your writing threatens to become drudgery, when your novel starts to drag, quit and begin another one. This tip, which has saved many a professional, is only one of the pat, ready-made solutions to all the problems that will ever face you as a writer.

Perhaps you have always wanted to be a writer but have never had the nerve to try. Perhaps you even doubt your ability to complete an entire novel. Don't be deterred. A novel is just a story that has been dragged out to at least 70,000 words. After all, if you can do your own divorce, you can certainly do your own novel (and probably have to make up less). Or maybe you feel that you could write a novel but that you do not have the time. Learn to write for short stretches. Roll your word processor into your bathroom. Nobody says you have to finish an entire novel in just a few weeks. Write a little at a time, even if it literally takes you months to finish. The effort will be worth your patience; the pecuniary rewards alone are enormous.

Or maybe you are even one of those misguided idealists (is there any other kind?) who feel unworthy of the reading audience. There is no more groundless and tragic reason for not writing than an exaggerated respect for the reading public. In truth, successful writing is principally a matter of catering to the tastes of an undiscriminating audience. Remember, the big money lies in writing for the average reader, that numerically plenitudinous individual with no memory, no attention span, and no desire to think about what he, she, or it reads. Your novel will be this person's intellectual meat.

All this book offers you, aside from the masterful prose of those who enter the Bulwer-Lytton Fiction Contest, is a handful of easy-to-master tips that will catapult you to the top of the best-seller lists. Before you get started, though, there are a few things you must know about support groups, those literary training wheels that some aspiring writers find convenient. If you think it will help to meet regularly with other writers to go over one another's manuscripts, to exchange ideas and consolations, then do not be embarrassed to do so—for a few weeks. However, you do need to take precautions.

To begin with, try to find a knowledgeable group. You will be able to tell right away if they know anything by the way they respond to your work. If they like your stuff, you will know that you have found a sensitive audience. If, on the other hand, they don't, you will have found a bunch of know-nothings or, worse, a coven of no-talent, envious backbiters. Even in the best of groups there is likely to be at least someone jealous of your talent who will find something to criticize in your writing. Do not be taken in by this.

A support group can be a legitimate help, but only if the other members do their work. You may find it useful to bounce your idea and inspirations off someone else, but only so long as you do not have to waste a lot of your time on their stuff. You need not feel guilty about this seeming one-sidedness. Pay just enough attention to pick up ideas. Most of the other members will not have your ability so the most they can hope for is that you will salvage something from their writing to put into publishable form. They should be flattered, really. After all, the people in your group will be able to trade someday on the fact that they knew you *when*. This acquaintance will gain them entry to other groups where they will be celebrities of a sort by pretending that they contributed to your success.

In sum, professional writing is an enormously rewarding career—monetarily, socially, and psychically. Think of the power at your fingertips to create characters, to give them language and personalities, to follow them around, to listen to their thoughts, to watch them undress. Can you think of another pastime that offers so many enticements?

1986 WINNER

~·~·~·~·~·~

The bone-chilling scream split the warm summer night in two, the first half being before the scream when it was fairly balmy and calm and pleasant, the second half still balmy and quite pleasant for those who hadn't heard the scream at all, but not calm or balmy or even very nice for those who did hear the scream, discounting the little period of time during the actual scream itself when your ears might have been hearing it but your brain wasn't reacting yet to let you know.

—*Patricia E. Presutti*
Lewiston, New York

1987 WINNER

~·~·~·~·~

The notes blatted skyward as the sun rose over the Canada geese, feathered rumps mooning the day, webbed appendages frantically pedaling unseen bicycles in their search for sustenance, driven by cruel Nature's maxim, "Ya wanna eat, ya gotta work," and at last I knew Pittsburgh.

—*Sheila B. Richter*
Minneapolis, Minnesota

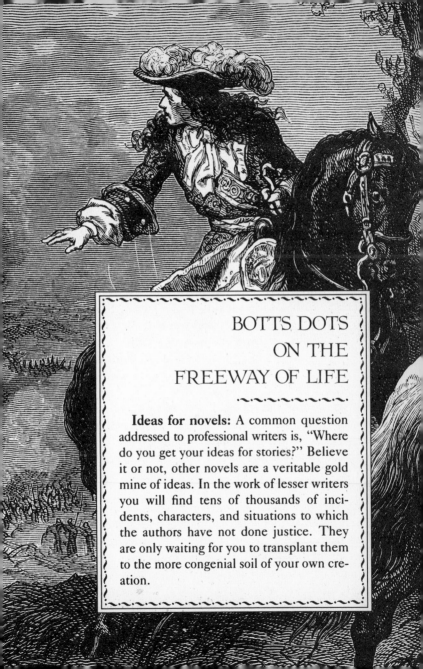

BOTTS DOTS
ON THE
FREEWAY OF LIFE

Ideas for novels: A common question addressed to professional writers is, "Where do you get your ideas for stories?" Believe it or not, other novels are a veritable gold mine of ideas. In the work of lesser writers you will find tens of thousands of incidents, characters, and situations to which the authors have not done justice. They are only waiting for you to transplant them to the more congenial soil of your own creation.

Mavis was a good woman—no doubt about it—thought Earl Himsley as he wheeled his Kenworth rig from the parking lot of the Gorman Gormay Diner where Mavis slung hash, onto the infinite stretch of Interstate 5; she was a curb, a guard rail, who kept him from straying into the wrong lane; she was his center divider, his arrangement of orange cones, indeed his very Botts dots on the Freeway of Life.

—*Nancy Wambach*
San Jose, California

As we lay supine in a rapture indigenous to springtime along the Northwest volcano coast, I gently stroked your nondairy creamy thigh as we reminisced about our recent interstate interface with a tulip-seeking traffic jam in Skagit Valley, a jam that at the time had caused you to comment on how "We are all like pink dogwood blossoms barking at a wind chime."

—*Robert L. Schlosser*
Seattle, Washington

It was spring, the season of resurrection, and the lilies broke free from the entombment of the oppressive earthen clods, then rose skyward like a host of Bantu spears in obeisance to aeons of genetic morphism.   —*Steven N. Spetz*
Kingston, Ontario, Canada

As she lay back on the sun-bussed beach, indifferently watching Brobdingnagian cauliflower florets of cumulus clouds scud languidly by in the cerulean sky, she recalled with bittersweet ambivalence that it was on just such a beach, on just such a day, that Jean-Claude first let her use his snorkel equipment.

—*Robert Carroll*
Glen Rock, New Jersey

The warm tropical sun caressed the golden Bermuda sand where Kimberly lay slathered in cocoa butter, welcoming its embrace and wallowing in the reverie while pounds of care melted away from the thighs of her psyche.

—*Geoffrey Eisen*
Honolulu, Hawaii

The restless ocean thrust forth a darkling wave which probed the stiffened corpse of the cormorant (whose parted beak lips pointed skyward as if to say, "Hey!" to the unheeding blue) with dispassionate fingers and carefully hefted the rotting mess in its cold, careless arms, inching it incrementally up the beach till it rested stoically by a discarded breath mint.

—*Jennifer C. Kemner*
Grandview, Missouri

She had never heard the word *pettifogger* before that steamy August evening when her mother, always a devout and quiet woman who showed anger in small furies of snapping her Spandoflex watch band until her wrist resembled flesh victimized by close and violent contact with a Portuguese man-of-war (or, at least, a hot griddle), sent her father from the porch with that epithet ringing on the night, its tones muffled by the humidity.   —*Kristen Kingsbury Henshaw*
Wakefield, Massachusetts

"You call this food!" shrieked Harold, and flung his plate against the wall, leaving the spaghetti as a clammy, quivering, glutinous mass that trembled and glistened and held together only a moment before beginning to disintegrate and drip, strand by gooey strand, to the tile below, while the warmed-over lasagna, glue-like, clung tight to the plaster wall and slowly,

voluptuously, oozed its way to the floor with a sickening gurgle, leaving behind it a thick, slimy, sticky track, like a huge slug overfed on ripe tomatoes.
—*Wanda Prather*
Severn, Maryland

On writers' notebooks: A writer's notebook can be an invaluable source of ideas, a place for recording details and scenes and characters. If you hang around coffee shops long enough, you should be able to get your hands on one. Eventually some would-be writer is going to go to the rest room and leave one behind.

The door, which was left open by the young, pert girl wearing a peasant blouse trimmed in Belgian lace with the laundry mark on the back and a bright full skirt with gaudy flowers in organized blotches, who reminded Raoul, the gardner, of that long-ago spring when he proved his manhood in a flowery—much like the flowers on the girl's dress (except that they were daisies, not roses)—field with a lady welder a few years his senior, but who was said to weld the straightest seams in the yard, even though she tended to be a bit careless with the excess flux falling on her steel-tipped shoes, blew shut.
—*Donald E. Gray*
Snellville, Georgia

The tender fact that her bare, soft shoulders were drawn slightly forward; the inviting fact that her pallid lips were even now roseate with a flush of palpable longing; the warming fact that her eyes seemed to glow with a gemlike yet supple flame; the electrifying fact that her murmuring voice was wrapping itself wetly around his name in a hastily repeated pattern; the hardening reality of the moment about to settle so unexpectedly but friskily upon them: all these brought his attention to a staggeringly specific point; but the mere fact that she was a female—this was what really cranked him.

—Tim Myers
Colorado Springs, Colorado

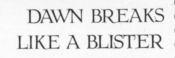

DAWN BREAKS
LIKE A BLISTER

How to open a novel: The purpose of your opening is to tame your readers, to let them know that they are in the company of someone far more sensitive, intelligent, and experienced than they are. You can accomplish this deftly with several pages of dense description and authorial commentary.

Dawn breaks like a blister, the sun rises like an egg in your Maypo, and the cry of the loons wafts over the water like a ruptured whoopee cushion—ah, home! to where a hundred crippled thoughts flap over the reedy morass of my youth, past the oleaginous pits of my adolescence to the bogs of my manhood.
—*Tom Goff*
Piedmont, California

The sun rose slowly, like a fiery fur ball coughed up uneasily onto a sky-blue carpet by a giant unseen cat.
—*Michael McGarel*
Park Forest, Illinois

The horizon coughed up the morning sun much as if Atlas had lowered the world from his mighty shoulders and given it the Heimlich maneuver. —*Bruce K. MacDonald*
Scarborough, Ontario, Canada

The sun came up like an undercooked egg, slimy around the edges like phlegm coughed up by a rummy with a month-old cold.
—*Susan Varno*
Peotone, Illinois

As the brutal dawn spat out the innocent new sun like a putrefying cherry tomato, Jake Byron shifted his position on the ice floe and decided it was time to reconsider his life, beginning with that day, not unlike this one, when he was born.
—*William Moseley*
Rockledge, Florida

It was a damp and drizzly day, not unlike the dark and dank interiors of some massive sinus cavity dripping, dripping incessantly, but never draining.   —*Vicki Paski-Nasser*
Houston, Texas

The coin rattled against the slot like a pebble in a Mixmaster; the handle clanked rhythmically on its gears; the tumblers slowly came to a halt, the first a bell, then another bell, then a third; the silver dollars tumbled joyfully into the tray; and Agnes sighed miserably, knowing it was turning into one of those nights when it would take her four hours to lose fifty bucks.   —*Jil McIntosh*
Oshawa, Ontario, Canada

Opening sentences: Good opening sentences should seize the reader the way a puppy seizes a rag bag—and shake the living daylights out of him (or her, whatever!).

Seeing the pouches, like leathern sacks filled with mayonnaise, under his eyes, she remembered that steamy night in Nairobi when Zagrib brought her the rear footpad of a lion preserved in a jar of gin and asked, "Memsahib, will you join me in an egg salad at the Crown and Lion?" and she had killed the response, "Okay, if you think there's room for both of us," that sprung to her lips.   —*M. E. Lockridge*
Los Alamos, New Mexico

Fiercely she struggled, like a weasel in the jaws of a terrier, twisting and straining, every muscle taut, knuckles white, and breaths coming in agonized gasps for what seemed like an eternity, until finally it was all over and once again Jane Svelte could think rational thoughts like, "Is wearing a girdle one size too small really worth the effort?"
—*Ron Leeming*
Edmonton, Alberta, Canada

He was, in a way, not unlike the car he drove: small, homely, and gutless; but like that car, an early-model Pinto, he had a latent tendency, when pushed too far or driven too hard, to explode.
—*Robert W. McConkey*
Scarborough, Ontario, Canada

Her flamethrower passion ignited his spent desire, like those little paper wrappers you see on bran muffins when you leave them in the oven too long.
—*Donald McLeod*
Sherman Oaks, California

The sea was utterly calm, like a vast bathroom mirror reflecting blue tile, with foam deposited by a flick of God's razor: the wake of a single vessel.
—*Donald K. King*
Oakland, California

The captain of the *Deliverance* scanned the ruffled zone beneath the crimson horizon, but all that met his eyes were the flotsam and jetsam that had once comprised the mighty schooner *Godspeed* but was now strewn randomly in large pieces across the gently rolling sea, like vomit floating on the surface of an infinite commode.
—*David Jarman*
Corvallis, Oregon

As the two lovers strolled along the beach, the setting sun glistened through the surf, fluoroscoping the undulating gelatin salad as it washed ashore, grotesque tangles of rotting kelp—finned kumquats strung like diseased Christmas tree lights on enema tubes—the fetic aroma attracting nervous mobs of little black insects.
—*Bill Stager*
Dayton, Ohio

With the sickening thud that a cloth sack filled with rabbit entrails makes when colliding with a concrete wall, the sack of rabbit entrails smashed into the wall behind me.
—*Trygve Lode*
Cherry Hills Village, Colorado

Jed was awed by the grandeur of this canyon as the raft once again hit white water and he fought to stay afloat with strength that came unbidden from deep, previously untapped sources, and marveled that a place so majestic, so imposing, could still look like a buttonhole next to his mother-in-law's mouth.
—*Mary Satterfield-Gilmer*
Champion, Michigan

Getting started: When you start a novel, you do not have to be settled yet on location, characters, conflicts, or themes. Simply listen to your creative imagination when it says, "Trust me!"

ALFRED
OF THE ARCTIC

Titles: Remember, the first words of your novel that anyone will read is the title, hence the imperative to compose a real grabber, like *Love's Flaming Groin*. One idea is to play on a famous expression: *Mightier Than the Pen*. Another idea is to use a cryptic title that cannot be understood until one reads the novel: *Turkey* or *Lemon*. (Sartre played with fire by entitling one novel *Nausea*.) Or you may want a subtle reference to an established classic: *To Kill a Titmouse*.

The fury of the arctic blizzard abated and allowed the aura of the aurora to pinwheel across his impassive features, touch briefly the anthracitic irises and reflect the specter of the force he feared second only to his stout spouse—the gigantic polar bear, whose intent was to devour this puny hunter defending a dead seal, destined to sustain his clamoring children and faithful though portly wife, even now experiencing severe hunger pangs within the chill confines of their sparsely outfitted igloo several hours by dogsled from his present precarious position, the thought of which caused his gallant, cholesterol-free heart to well within his parka-clad chest, his frigid digits to tighten around the rigid shaft (of his hunting spear), his nose to flare and run, and his cracked, cold-ravaged lips to spread, revealing a gap-toothed grin as he, Alfred E. Noomanikpuk, shouted, "What, me worry?"

(from *Alfred of the Arctic*) —*James P. Rudhoe*
Prudhoe Bay, Alaska

Ukluk returned to the distant ice fields where he had left his aged and sickly grandmother to die twenty years ago and found her huddled in the snow, shivering and eating a butchered polar bear amid a vast mountain of slaughtered walruses, wolves, and other skinned and half-eaten bears, and turned sadly away, pitying her futile attempts to forestall the inevitable, noticing with some anguish the hostile glance she had tossed in his direction. —*J. J. Solari*
Burbank, California

By the fourth day of the auto tour across the vast Indian countryside over wretched washboard roads, Neville found himself despising the land and its natives; and when the wiz-

ened, ashen-skinned beggar yelled, "Swine!" in perfectly clear English as Neville whizzed past, he felt compelled to turn his head to retort, "Savage!" and thereby had insufficient time to brake the car as it rounded the bend and ran headlong into the largest pig he had ever seen.　　　—*John Bulger*
Missoula, Montana

I knew then that it had been a mistake to sell our scrap metal, as the Kamikaze pilot crawled free of the smoking, wreckage-strewn carrier deck and came at us with American razor blades taped to his fingers.　　　—*Leon D. Bayer*
Los Angeles, California

Noting the nervous countenance of a new recruit toward the advancing hordes of howling Gallic barbarians, the Centurion Effacacious whispered a few steadying words, in the manner of old soldiers throughout eternity, saying, "Aye, lad, that blond giant leaping and shouting there in his berserk barbarian frenzy of rage will not look half so fearsome with his mouth twisted into a rictus of pain and bellowing his death agony because the head of your javelin is buried deep in his Gallic guts and its protruding shaft is oscillating up and down, up and down, up and down in harmonic resonance in short arcs of ever-decreasing length."　　　—*Robert D. Norris, Jr.*
Tulsa, Oklahoma

"Arr, Matey!" bellowed the first mate from the bridge, "I'm a warnin' ye that if I ever sees ye on deck with a shirt on, in direct violation of our dress code, to which ye swore before signin' onto me crew as a full-blooded pirate, I'll haul ye and hang yer mangled remains from the mast to dry in the midday

sun, swayin' back 'n' forth, back 'n' forth with the gentle
rockin' motion of the ship."   —*David Morrell*
                                                 Madison, Alabama

It takes nerves of steel and hands of iron to wrestle the big
'gators, I mean the really big honkers, the ones big as '57
Buicks, only uglier, not those pitiful little show lizards that
you see at roadside stands, and it's something that you're born
to do, and maybe born able to do, something in your blood
and bone, something in your sinews and thews, something in
your liver and lights, something that goes pancreas-deep, a
need, a hunger, a kinship to the great, cold-blooded water
dragons—or so I've heard, although I wouldn't really know,
being a fry cook in Butte myself.   —*Ray C. Gainey*
                                         Indianapolis, Indiana

Through the smoke and carnage, I beheld the valiant Major
Hawkins—a dashing figure with steely-blue eyes and strong,
broad shoulders; and whose smiling countenance, smeared as
it was with mud and battle soot, would have inspired heroism
in the weakest of men—standing up from the trench, raising
his saber to the heavens and shouting, "Come on, lads, they
couldn't hit an elephant at this dist—. . . !"
                                         —*Warren Walker*
                                         Merriam, Kansas

"Drats!" Lance exclaimed as he glanced out of the window
at the frozen tundra far below when he realized that he had
forgotten to pack his Water-Pik and therefore faced the very
real possibility that the scrambled eggs he had so eagerly wolfed
down earlier in the flight might remain lodged in the cavernous

sockets left by the recent extraction of his wisdom teeth until he returned to civilization some six months hence.

—*Craig Sweat*
Smyrna, Georgia

Shivalingam Dhoti, faithful servant of the English sahib, screamed with horror, "English sahib, for the love of Vishnu, look out for that tiger trap!" but Lord Folderol-Pugh had already fallen through the plantain leaves.

—*Mary Lee Ward*
Chicago, Illinois

Coughing, spitting, and gasping for breath, Reggie surfaced in the cesspool, desperately treading the foul, murky liquid as he tried to remember from which direction he had heard the splash of his .357 Magnum, which had slipped from his hand as the baron pushed him from the helicopter.

—*Caroline Luna*
Oklahoma City, Oklahoma

Writing adventure stories: In writing adventure stories, there is no excuse for gratuitously introducing lewd and lascivious scenes, graphic and detailed depictions of prolonged sex between extraordinarily attractive characters, except for purely artistic purposes—such as giving the reader a little R and R between killings.

On this Godforsaken speck of land in the middle of nowhere, with no sounds save the pounding of the waves and the raucous cry of gulls to break the silence, with no company save one hairy, disgusting goat, Crusoe's days passed like kidney stones, until finally, inevitably, the goat began to look good to him.
—*Wayne D. Worthey*
Washington, D.C.

It didn't matter to Gordon that he couldn't outrun the enraged mother grizzly; all he had to do was outdistance his chubby hiking partner, Fred.
—*David Willingham*
Georgetown, Tennessee

"I'll never get this tuxedo back to 42nd Street Rentals in time!" he thought as he twisted to look up at the two lady Hells Angels who had just pitched him headfirst out of the plane into the warm Peruvian morning sky high above the city of Lima. . . .
—*David A. Schubert*
Dedham, Massachusetts

"He may be Lord of the Jungle," mused Jane as she took advantage of the darkness of the African night, the insistent drone of the buzzing insects, and the potency of the mango milk they had just consumed at dinner to change her mate's voice range to soprano with her hunting knife, "but that's the last time he'll make a monkey out of me!"
—*Janet M. Kaul*
Redwood City, California

"Well, old bean, looks like we're done for this time!" said famed explorer Reginald Fozworth with a stiff upper lip, a childhood affliction which had proved particularly embarrassing when kissing girls or playing the French horn.

—*Jan M. Meriwether*
APO Miami, Florida

Heat and pain coursed through Cohn's flesh like an angry bull swimming the English Channel, and Cohn, straining manfully against the thongs of doom that bound him, and somewhat hurt by the dawning recognition that Muffie had betrayed him, could see, from his vantage point atop a pyre of burning branches, the grins on the faces of the Ibojwa elders, whose teeth were sharpened to fine points, as was the pencil of the their leader (for this was to be the tribe's first recorded human feast, and Cohn the meal). —*Bruce Goldman*
San Francisco, California

The morning breeze of the perpetually still jungle wafted softly through the suddenly opened louvers as the considerate and faithful servant, Sri Lamsri, placed the familiar breakfast tray across the bed and lifted the polished metal cover from the dish, revealing not the customary curried eggs, crisp kidney, and a side of cottage fries, but a .487 Hammacher-Schlemmer police special equipped with Pinot-Citron silencer, plugging Melissa five times—*wham! wham! wham! wham! wham! wham!*—through her slender gut, purring softly in the kind voice she had known all her life, "Compliments, little missy, of the Sri Leduc People's Liberation Army and Martyrs Beneficial Fund." —*Arnold Rosenfeld*
Austin, Texas

Her eyes sparkling with excitement, young Bess dreamily contemplated the thrilling adventures that no doubt lay before her as she watched the drearily pastoral village of her birth recede into the distance until only the smoke, lazily drifting upward from the burning homes of her friends and family, could be seen, and the terrified screams of the sorely beset villagers were a mere whisper, barely audible over the grunting respirations of the filthy, hulking Viking who was carrying her like a sack of potatoes to the waiting longship.

—*Lisa D. Winters*
Kansas City, Missouri

His coat bulging like a rotting cat with maggots, Kevy Honeyman, his too-pretty lips involuntarily pouted, stumbled up to a border guard in that two-bit, fourth-class, third-world banana-land country, beads of Roman-candle sweat popping from his brows as he nervously eyed the guard's open shirt, which revealed a mat of jungle-musky hair that Kevy would come to know all too well in the ensuing months, and trying to act casual, he squeaked out in a crackling Freudian falsetto slip-of-doom, "Golly, it's raining cats and hashish out there!"

—*Glenn Bering*
Ann Arbor, Michigan

Splintering the pus-lizards's brittle skull between pitted molars, Baron Painphagg the Putrescent cursed with dripping breath the radiant cold that bored deep into his aching Bragorfian bones like crazed bloodlice, and wondered for the fourteenth time why in the Half-dozen Horrible Hells his sordid band of grimy cutthroats had insisted on marauding this far north, in the entirely godforsaken wastes of Nas Teegrode where the limp sun dangled in the leprous sky like a bruised penny.

—*David W. Sisk*
Atlanta, Georgia

"YOUR PLAN IS BRILLIANT, VON RYSBROECK!"

Writing police procedurals: There is no substitute for authentic on-the-line experience with law-enforcement agencies. How does a civilian writer acquire such experience? Fortunately, most school districts have a program for volunteer crossing guards. In your yellow raincoat and Sam Browne belt, you will be protecting the innocent and enforcing the statutes on potential lawbreakers—the very essence of police work.

"Your plan is brilliant, Von Rysbroeck!" I admitted, calmly aware of the whitening knuckle on his gun hand. "But I'm afraid you have overlooked one thing—namely, that where all beneficiaries of a trust established before 1949 reside, during a taxation year, in one country other than Canada and all amounts included in computing income of the trust for the taxation year were received from persons resident in that country, no tax is payable to a beneficiary as income of or from the trust; anyway, there is no eighth metatarsal bone, and furthermore, you have no gun."

—*Patrick S. Finnegan*
Victoria, British Columbia, Canada

Detectives Third-Class Bill Dougherty and Frank Holloman, unwilling to return to the station from the false comfort of Ray's, were getting drunker by the hour, knowing that Chief Boswell would be livid when he learned that after months of surveillance, they had allowed the entire ring responsible for the city's trade in illegal designer suppositories to slip through their fingers.

—*Joseph Peter Myers*
Riverside, California

It was the kind of neighborhood, Mulcahey thought, where the buildings existed only to hold the shadows apart and the puddles together, where if you saw a doorway *without* a furtive figure skulking in it it meant you weren't looking hard enough, the kind of neighborhood where the only thing your shoulder blades wondered was *when* someone would try to stick a knife between them, the kind of neighborhood, he concluded with a shiver, checking the safety on his .457 Magnum, where they put Greyhound bus terminals.

—*"Dr. Dan" Villani*
Long Beach, California

The report from the snub-nosed .38 still whined in the corners of the room as the sleek lead projectile nestled in the wet folds of Dwight's cerebral cortex, causing him relexively to squeeze the remote channel selector until his face crashed forward on the aging Formica, leaving his Sylvania tuned on the cosmic riddle that is Phil Donahue.   —*Steve Volstad*
Aurora, Colorado

As he sat in his study ruminating on Othello's final "to die upon a kiss" speech, and thrilling in his palpitating bosom over last night's tryst with Home Ec teacher Prunella Danish while her buns were warming in the oven for the PTA meeting going on in the gym, a bullet no bigger than a black farkleberry broke open a small hole at the base of the skull of Mr. Fenton Smalley of Cherryville High's English department, and, in the .05 of a second before his head struck his desk with the dull thud of a full oat sack, Fenton gasped, his wife laughed, and the bullet in his brain passed like a skewer through shish-kebabbed beef.   —*Larry R. Isitt*
Coeur d'Alene, Idaho

The professor lay on the floor in a widening pool of blood as Detective Johnson knelt by his side in time to hear the victim gasp, "It was . . . it was . . . Richard Keller, 1295 Maple Street, area code 691/555-6954, aaah . . ."
—*Richard W. O'Bryan*
Perrysburg, Ohio

John lay tied and gagged in the backseat without any idea of where they were taking him, but he knew there were tele-

phone poles—telephone poles whizzing past a never-ending row of crucifixes.
                                        —Pat Shaver
                                        Norman, Oklahoma.

When I walked into the room and saw the twisted, dead corpse lying lifeless on the blood-soaked carpet, I wanted and needed to cry in the worst sort of way, but I couldn't—a sort of lachrymal constipation—so I lightly stepped over the body in its gruesome repose and walked over to the desk to play with the adding machine until help arrived.
                                        —Pamela Wylder
                                        Bloomington, Illinois

Insider tip: Certain things authentic cops never do, such as pick up murder weapons with a handkerchief. In reality, policemen are extremely fastidious about their sartorial accessories. Hence, if the weapon is a large-bore handgun, a police detective will pick it up by inserting his little finger down the barrel (ideally, not the same finger he always licks to taste unknown substances, even when investigating poisonings).

Had the fiend who unleased the truckload of steel ball bearings from the top of the exit ramp been driven by dark Malthusian visions of overpopulation, by misogyny gone mad, or by overwhelming guilt over the number of cookies he had eaten in March, Lieutenant Arvid wondered, wing-tipping

carefully through the crimson-and-green remains of Girl Scout Troop #257.
　　　　　　　　　　　　　　—*Patricia Thomas*
　　　　　　　　　　　　　　Arlington, Massachusetts

When I found Napoleon, our new butler on release from Saint Hadhisdruthers, the asylum for the criminally insane, standing over Uncle Nelson's dead body and holding a bloody knife in one hand and a smoking gun in the other, I shrieked, "Who did it?"
　　　　　　　　　　　　　　—*Marlene Murphy Sheehan*
　　　　　　　　　　　　　　Southport, Connecticut

It was noon, and I was eating yesterday's breakfast at the Château Amour, an antiquated two-story love temple of white painted brick, where the patrons resembled a Barnum and Bailey sideshow, the men vile and unctuous, the women painted in garish pastels and dressed in leather, female gladiators in a sexual arena, a microcosm of life in a social colostomy bag, and pondered my depressingly short career as a personal image consultant and *vers libre* poet.
　　　　　　　　　　　　　　—*Donald G. Olmstead*
　　　　　　　　　　　　　　Pittsburgh, Pennsylvania

Frank, driving slowly, tenderly caressing his wife Johanna, who lay beside him, and thinking of all that he liked about her: her long, thick sandy hair with natural glittering blond highlights; her bright green eyes that couldn't lie; her success and charm that made women envy her and men seek her; her easy way with absolutely everyone, suddenly realized that things could get very sticky if he didn't get rid of her body.
　　　　　　　　　　　　　　—*Theo Baer*
　　　　　　　　　　　　　　Montreal, Quebec, Canada

Roger Helmsley's craggy face quickly took on the pained expression of someone who has just been appointed junior partner in the law firm of Manson, Hinkley, Berkowitz, and Speck, as the man seated across him—the cherubic-looking new Bronx District Attorney—informed him that he had been "invited" downtown to shed some light on how a pinkie finger and an eyeball belonging to his missing wife had both suddenly surfaced as Cracker Jack prizes at a Yankee Stadium refreshment stand.
—*Frances X. Brady*
New York, New York

There within the dingy, ominous, and somber gray walls of the police station, as she was being booked as an accessory to murder, Charlotte Ferris thought about how, just a few fleetingly short months ago, she had innocently and jokingly told Dolores Payne, the battered and abused wife she counseled as a volunteer at a women's shelter, how she, Dolores, could rid herself of her violent and hateful husband by buying swollen, oozing cans of food and feeding the contents to him, and about how she, Charlotte Ferris, the middle-class, middle-of-the-road, relatively happy suburban wife of status-conscious, successful wicker basket importer Emmet Ferris, could never have known that Dolores would actually do it.

—*Myra Reisman*
Commack, New York

Noble Henry Sontag's head burst with a resounding *splat!* at the base of the clock tower, leaving us—sadly—Jeffrey Withers as our protagonist.
—*Don Webb*
Austin, Texas

I viciously splintered the dragon-green door of the scruffy Chinese restaurant with my steel-toed size-twelve brogan, rocketed into the soy-scented interior with my custom-made, onyx-gripped .38 belching a litany of death, watched with gory satisfaction as claret fountained from the tailored silk jackets of the pair of cretinous swine who had so wantonly destroyed my every hope, my every dream, and then heard the proprietor, Ho Ching, speak in bland, inscrutable tones, "With two you get egg roll."

—*Robert V. Wright*
Encino, California

Maintaining suspense: One secret to keeping your reader involved is to end each chapter on a point of suspense, with something dramatic about to occur:

"He leaned back in his armchair and closed his eyes. He just knew that something was bound to happen eventually, maybe even soon, and it probably wouldn't be very nice, either."

This is real tension, so exercise restraint in ratcheting up even more suspense.

LYTTONY I

On visualization: Visualization is a keen way to get your novel started. Lean back in your chair, close your eyes, and imagine that someone is approaching your door, someone in a uniform, a blue uniform. This person is slipping something into your mailbox. You open the door and take it out. It is a letter, a letter from your agent. It contains a royalty check. The check is in six figures, *before the decimal point*. Now, doesn't that make you ready to start writing?

"God, I'm tired," thought Jim-Bob as he jammed the seventeen-speed road ranger into double-compound fifth gear and gracefully swung the big rig into the right lane, effortlessly flattening the front end of a '69 LTD, making it resemble a giant green metallic spatula with wheels on the handle.
(from *Life Between the Ditches*)   —T. L. Bulgrin
                                                      Owen, Wisconsin

He thought it could never happen in real life, but when Mr. Timmons opened his closet and saw three large, red, glowing eyes staring back at him from behind the neat rows of his plastic sock racks, he found himself trying to gather up speed by running in place for about five seconds, his feet all a-blur, before rocketing out of the bedroom—just as he had always seen it happen in cartoons.

                                                    —*Peter Nemarich*
                                                     New Haven, Connecticut

Rodney finally realized, as he lay there in the dust, looking like a melted ice cream bar on a sidewalk in a hot July sun, made that way by a quite sudden and unexpected stampede of elephants, that Ethel, his wife, had been lying to him when she had said his horoscope had read, "Go to the circus today and reap rich rewards!" and, though Rodney was never one to say anything bad about a person, he thought it very strange that, when he said he was going, Ethel had insisted he wear peanut oil cologne she had bought him for Christmas.

                                                    —*Richard W. Brown*
                                                     Scottville, Michigan

Long, long ago, in a village outside of Philly, lived a dwarf and a witch, husband and wife respectively, whose only ar-

guments in life were that she was too stubborn to dance back-
wards and he was too short to make her.
                              —*Jo. J. Molnar*
                              Huntington Beach, California

Cletus had an uneasy feeling about eating at a joint called
the Road Kill Café, but he was hungry and still miles from
Memphis, so he swung his rig onto the gravel lot beneath the
glowing red neon possum.   —*David Willingham*
                              Georgetown, Tennessee

"Help! help!" Ruth Rambles shouted, unaware that her
male companion for the afternoon's 1st Baptist Kite Fly had
become entangled in some discarded piano wire while running
to lift his Blue Dragon off the dappled pasture, or that the
vicious hound's lips were caught on the barbed wire fence.
                              —*Thomas Sullivan*
                              Lathrup Village, Michigan

I first began to suspect that I was going mad the night I
woke from a troubled reverie to discover that my hairpiece,
missing from its customary stand on my bedside table, was in
the kitchenette, locked in an amorous cinch with my pet ham-
ster, Stanley.   —*Gerald Bowen*
                              London, England

Ram was what his buddies always called him, since he had
an eye for the ladies far and wide, always finding the grass
greener on the other side of the desert, although today his
good ship *Lady Luck* appeared to have run aground as he found
himself stuck fast in a thicket, distracted first by the amazing
scene of a bearded old man about to stick a knife into a little

boy, then by a cloying celestial voice that boomed, almost shattering his left eardrum, "Abraham, spare your son and take Ram instead!"
—*David M. Knipe*
Madison, Wisconsin

"This is almost worth the high blood pressure!" he thought as yet another mosquito exploded.
—*Richard Patching*
Calgary, Alberta, Canada

As she snapped on the Lava Lamp in what she still lovingly called "The Nursery," noticing through the clouds of cigar smoke and primal churnings of the Boingers Album on the turntable that the heads of the youngsters groping on the couch were bobbing and weaving like two flamingos in a food processor, two thoughts raced simultaneously through Mother's mind, the first concerning the economy of the Puberty-Pronto breakfast cereal she had been serving, and the second being, "Is it time to change their diapers?"
—*David A. Schubert*
Dedham, Massachusetts

More on ideas for stories: Your best friend is the wastepaper basket—not yours, somebody else's, preferably another writer's.

Mildred retched violently when she saw Steingrimum, the swarthy exchange student from Iceland who favored Tibetan literature and Falkland Island polka music, impale Archibald, her favorite gray-and-white Norwegian Forest cat who only recently returned home from Dr. Kit Kitchard's Kitty Klinic following surgery for removal of a four-pound hair ball, with a shish-kebab skewer and then casually roast him over a cedarwood flame which glowed peacefully in the fireplace.

—*Michael W. Paris*
Westover, West Virginia

Ernest Hemingway had been his hero ever since he was belched out of his mother's angry, belligerent womb.

—*Rainy Gage*
Olympia, Washington

"*Nada* is *nada* is *nada* is *nada*," muttered Ernest in bed, puffing on his hard black cigarette, when Gertrude, holding his hand, implored him, "When I said, 'There is no there there,' I was only talking about Oakland."

—*John M. Hendry*
Van Nuys, California

I was very hungry and the meal was good and I drank a bottle of Capri and a bottle of St. Estephe and a bottle of grappa and a bottle of the fake chianti, after which I felt splendid on the veranda, watching Japonica bathe in the cold stream, the one with the good hard tangible little pebbles at the bottom. —*Norman Burnett*
Alexandria, Virginia

Jennifer Pennypacker's pooch pushing a shopping cart down the razor-thin aisle may have been an unlikely sight, but as his mistress, if not an outright workaholic, was something more

than a mere "social worker," Rufus had resigned himself to purchasing his own victuals, and flinty old Mr. Naterbee, his aching foot tap-tap-tapping like Ray Bolger choreographing the Anvil Chorus while the stodgy Lhasa Apso methodically counted out change, wondered casually whether the banker-lady's pet would be able to spring for the difference were the store ever to price its Ken-L rations, currently a loss leader, a bit closer to market value. —*Bruce Goldman*
San Francisco, California

"Jiminy Gryllidae!" exclaimed Pinocchio gratuitously, as he accidentally ran over and smashed into splinters Woody One-feather, the cigar-store Indian who, twenty years earlier, had set fire to his father's cobbler's shop, seduced his wife the good fairy, murdered his pet cricket with a shoe, and fled across the ocean to open the tobacco emporium at which Pinocchio had just now been planning to stop and buy some matches. —*Ann Rhodes Conley*
Pittsburgh, Pennsylvania

Marvin Furdblossom conceived such a great admiration for the many wonderful inventions of Thomas Edison, probably because he (Furdblossom) had been dandled on his (Edison's) knee at the age of three (Edison's knee was, in fact, sixty-five at the time), that he (Marvin) later became the first to undertake the perilous solo crossing of the Atlantic in his (both Edison's and Marvin's) phonograph, a journey which ended in disaster, no doubt because it (the phonograph) was over-laden by wax cylinders, and because its large horn was aero-dynamically unstable in the wind sheer two miles above the

town of Menlo Park, New Jersey, his (Marvin Furdblossom's) boyhood home and final resting place.*
(* Thomas Edison was raised in Menlo Park, California.)

—Brian Holmes
San Jose, California

SAMMY SLUGS
FIRST DAY OF SCHOOL

Writing for children: Remember that children experience most of the same emotions as adults—envy, greed, fear, hostility, resentment, vindictiveness. The only difference is that they are usually too short to do anything about them.

It was Sammy Slug's first day of school, and was he ever excited!—because he'd meet lots of other little worms, but he had to watch out for salt crossing the street on his way to school, his mother said, because if the patrol slug waved him and his glob of little friends across the busy, dangerous street that had been salted because of the snow, before Sammy knew it his little body would be sucked dry, and his poor mama would never see Sammy drag his slime across his doorstep again.
                                                —*Enid Shomer*
                                                Gainesville, Florida

Peabo, the cat, washed his fur in the warm sunlight that steamed through the window, thinking to himself as he licked his soiled paws, "Why, it's not so bad having a baby in the house," and then coughed up a hair ball and bits of a rattle.
                                                —*Merle Lee Pugh*
                                                Arispe, Iowa

Once upon a perfectly marvelous hot summer afternoon, Beatrice, the bluebottle fly, dressed her two young sons, Kevin and Trevor, in their nattiest blue blazers and paisley ascots, and took them down to the river to feed on a pile of putrefying fish guts that had been decomposing on the bank for nearly a week.
                                                —*Murray J. Munro*
                                                Edmonton, Alberta, Canada

Cunning little Bunny Bumper discovered that new summer peas were so much to his liking that he sat in the garden and ate and ate until his cunning little tummy got bigger and bigger and just exploded, propelling peas through the air with the

force of a shotgun blast and blowing a hole in the transmission of Farmer Frick's Ford.
(from *Dappled Days at Dismal Farm* by Fecundia Hare)
—*Mary Anthony*
Grand Rapids, Michigan

"Darn old duck!" the rodent shrieked squeakily as he triggered his .38, filling the air with soft white feathers, the odor of fresh blood and gunpowder, and ruining a perfectly good sailor suit. —*The Reverend William F. Charles*
St. Louis, Missouri

Bunny Wunny jumped out of bed on a bright and beautiful morning in May and put on his little blue trousers and his little red shirt with the yellow buttons, humming cheerfully as he washed behind his big floppy ears and combed his soft brown fur until it shone—little suspecting that before the sun set in the western sky he would be lying in Farmer Bob's ditch, his neck broken by the cold steel of a patented vermin trap. —*Brant Boucher*
Florenceville, New Brunswick, Canada

While little Harold crouched snickering maniacally behind the door, Eloise tumbled end over end down the stairs, like a giant pink-and-white Slinky toy, bones snapping like brittle toothpicks every time she hit another step.
—*Mary T. Hollifield, ATSL*
Rossville, Georgia

> Thanks to the state of our national literacy, there is a wider audience than ever for children's books.

As Annabel stood at the crossroads with the wet nose of Dodo—her pet dog and faithful companion—nervously peeking out of the picnic basket clutched tightly to her gingham-clad groin, and gazing with great puzzlement at the signpost sticking out of the pink-and-orange bubble-gum bushes that pointed to such curious places as "Anywhere," "Somewhere," and "Nowhere," she had little inkling that the strange and bizarre adventures to follow would all turn out to be a dream and that, when she woke, Aunt Murilla would still be sitting in the rocking chair on the stoop paring her toenails with the apple corer.
　　　　　　　　　　　　　　　—Michael Yeaman
　　　　　　　　　　　　　　　Tyne and Wear, England

Once upon a time there was a naughty little girl—just about your age—named Jennifer, and she was so naughty that finally her mommy said, "No wonder your *real* mommy and daddy left you in the hospital to be adopted! And I'm so glad you're not really *my* little girl (even though all this time you thought you were), because now I can take you back to the hospital and leave you there, and *maybe* someone else will want to adopt you—somebody mean, who likes to spank little girls."
　　　　　　　　　　　　　　　—Cynthia Conyers
　　　　　　　　　　　　　　　Aguanga, California

Little Joey had been busily playing by himself all morning long in the great hall that led to his mother's powdery boudoir, when suddenly he let fall his toy monkey, and in childhood's loveliest voice yelled, "Ma, Kitty just hocked a lunger on the credenza!"
—*John Geoffrey Alnutt*
Brooklyn, New York

The ugly little duckling sat by the edge of the pond and cried and cried and cried and cried, little realizing that one day he would grow up to be a fine, beautiful, elegant, gourmet duck "Rouennaise" served to the beautiful little princess of all the land.
—*James Sheldon Averbeck*
Cleveland, Ohio

The children in the studio audience were at first stunned, then bewildered, and finally wildly enthusiastic as Waldo the Clown, departing from the usual format of *Waldo's Candy Tree-house Show*, suddenly turned and pounced on Barky, the Wonder Dog, and beat him until he became incontinent.
—*Chris J. Graber*
St. Louis, Missouri

Mary Merryweather knelt among the spring flowers, cast a last loving look around her tiny garden, and sadly announced to her adorable children, "Our money is gone; pack your bags because Mom's splitting to the Coast and you brats are going to the orphanage."
—*Michael Miller*
Clovis, California

Nuggles the Whump-Whump bird flew quietly above the wonderful greenness of Happy-Tree Meadow, eagerly awaiting the cheerful humming that always signaled the beginning

of the Gubbywub Parade and Picnic, which annually provided the Whump-Whumps with enough Gubbywub fur and flesh to last the entire winter.   —*Bruce K. MacDonald*
Scarborough, Ontario, Canada

As a bunny, Oscar realized that his career options were severely limited to eating grass and reproducing, but he would not abandon his dreams of medical school.

—*David Morrell*
Madison, Alabama

On writing for children and adolescents: What does it take to create a children's novel? The chapters must be suited to the attention spans of today's youngsters. In a page and a half a chapter must resolve the action interrupted at the end of the previous chapter, advance the larger plot, repeat the characters' names, deal with any subplots, and then begin another crisis. As for ending the story satisfactorily, let the principal characters get what they want and see that all the blocking figures are crushed. This is also a good way to conclude adult fiction.

Cindy left today and I whined and cried imagining what it would be like if she decided never to return, or if the bus that took her away should lose its brakes and fly off the edge of some cliff, killing every person on board, or if she should slip in Mary Baskin's bathtub, breaking her neck and dying instantly, never coming back to hold me in her arms and scratch my belly, and never again to feed me those treats that I like so much because they taste just like real beef, and real chicken, and real liver—but at least her mother's here.

—*Brian Collins*
Ottawa, Ontario, Canada

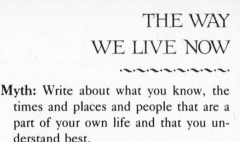

THE WAY
WE LIVE NOW

Myth: Write about what you know, the times and places and people that are a part of your own life and that you understand best.

Reality: This is fine advice for sex therapists and residents of Beirut or Belfast, but for most of us, who live in boring times and places and who have boring acquaintances and dull jobs, this is a recipe for failure. Nobody wants to hear about the experiences of a box boy in Spokane. Do yourself a favor and get subscriptions to *National Geographic* and *Soldier of Fortune*. You will learn about exotic locales and feats of derring-do, and you will also get some tips from the swell writing.

Stanislaus Smedley, a man always on the cutting edge of narcissism, was about to give his body and soul to a back-alley sex-change surgeon—to become the woman he loved.

—*John L. Orman*
Albuquerque, New Mexico

Up one aisle and down another, through the jungle of gustatory delights, she vainly sought to control the wheels of the stubborn steel vehicle, but slithering along the floor and crawling up the sides of the cart-gone-mad was a caloric convocation of marauding Mint Milanos, M&M's, Mystic Mints, and a veritable Galilee of foil-packed Sara Lee which propelled her inexorably down the wind-tunnel line with frozen fish sticks and Lean Cuisine wherein resided the Holy Grail, that black-and-white landscape that froze the very membranes of her tortured taste buds, two little words panting in the vapors of the pulsating Freon pump, "Dove Bar . . . Dove Bar . . . Dove Bar . . ."

—*Peggy Lee Scott*
Berkeley, California

It was a remarkable transformation, agreed Eunice-Ann Beezer, her nearsighted eyes darting from one photograph prominently displayed on the reception desk-cum-makeup-tray of the Chrysalis Beauty Salon and Finishing School (the very inscription she had just scrawled in her spidery hand on the check blank before her) to the other and back again, imagining the day "thirty-eight short weeks" hence when she, too, would emerge from the pores-you-could-hide-pennies-in homeliness of "Before" to achieve the timeless beauty of the "Professionally Unretouched After."

—*Helen Van Dongen*
Toronto, Ontario, Canada

Celebrity Bio: Like, I sincerely believe I'm no better than anybody else in the sense that I was born and all, but maybe luckier and with more determination, but a person catapulted into the Public's eye whether the Public likes it or not has got to realize how that makes him or her into a leader, be it political or whatever, so in a way I'd be heavily derelict if I didn't tell the Public the simple facts of (1) how to vote right and (2) how I'm on to something really heavily Metaphysically Correct which all of my fans as my equals have just *got* to know about and embrace or else be doomed for eternity as I know it, if you see what I mean.   —*Sheila Turnage*
Farmville, North Carolina

As she examined the deep purple welts on the inside of her thighs, ran her fingers over the bruises on her ribs, probed the ugly crimson scabs on the bottom of her feet, and painfully caressed her torn triceps, she knew that before dawn she would sneak into the bedroom and kill her aerobics dance instructor.
—*Frank H. Surpless*
Eagle River, Wisconsin

The chilling zephyr that raised a score or more goose bumps on Tawny's milk-white skin and caused them to nearly burst through her skintight Spandex shorts also wafted serenely through her blond, perfumed tresses as she jogged uninhibitedly along the deserted beach, as yet sublimely ignorant that the slight twinge she had felt that morning in her remaining tooth would soon spell the end to her promising and lucrative career as a hole puncher at Barney's Fit-Right Belt Emporium.
—*Jack Cannon*
Cincinnati, Ohio

There are times when everything loses its flavor, nothing tastes good, and things are generally a drag, so thought Newton McFarland as he threw his briefcase forcefully across the room—noting with satisfaction that his paper on "Recommendations for Control Administration for Inter-exchange Carrier Network Surveillance and Routing Control Administration" went flying like a rupped-up psychotic fiber optics cable—"Damn the Telecommunications Industry," he cursed, "I've got to jump off this gerbil treadmill and go bag a mountain!"

—*Ginger Gilcrease*
San Francisco, California

"This is the end!" lamented Bridget as she hung upside down and naked with a "Kiss me, I'm Irish" sign taped to her posterior, from the single fluorescent light in the visiting football team's locker room after the most embarrassing loss (20–0, ten safeties) to arch-rival high school, Our Lady of the Immaculate Reception, and prayed that they would not recognize her as the cheerleader who sacrificed their mascot, Billy the Miracle Goat, at the beginning of the third quarter.

—*Shannon Walker*
Redwood City, California

Flushing the seventeenth and last of his son Jason's toy robots down the upstairs john, Roger Watkins watched the spiral of blue water recede and reflected sulkily on the probability that this event would later be evoked as evidence of childhood deprivation, thereby earning Jason points at cocktail parties and in various women's bedrooms well into the twenty-first century.

—*Pamela Beck*
Fresno, California

On writing blocks: There may be times when you will be sitting in front of your typewriter or word processor, eyes glazed, fingers frozen, ears ringing, the tip of your nose numb, unable to write. Do not lose confidence or construe this as a reflection on your essential creativity. You are probably having a stroke.

It cost them $785 to discover that the twins, at only two years, could operate scissors, and that their neighbor's ratty old coat (which was called Gentle Ben and Sasquatch by unkinder neighbors) was, indeed, a mink.

—*Kristen Kingsbury Henshaw*
Wakefield, Massachusetts

Firmly, almost indignantly, Thornton Entwhistle straightened his toupee and checked his lapels for stray specks of lint as he stood in front of the firmly closed mahogany door and again rehearsed his request for a legal pad all his own.

—*Jim Menard*
Rochester, New York

The excitement had reached the fever pitch, all eyes straining skyward, whilst the early-rising throngs, the musicians, and the dancers in native costume eagerly awaited the annual event, for this was "Saint Olaf's Day" when for the past year and a half, the starlings have historically returned to the Murphy Brothers' feed lot near Oxnard, California.

—*Byron Castle*
Mill Valley, California

Winifred slammed the ornate French doors of her penthouse apartment, stamped her rose-spiked heels across the marble foyer to her mirrored bedroom, where she collapsed onto her pink satin coverlet and thought that life on the streets was too dangerous and perhaps being called Miss Winifred by a roomful of kindergartners was not all that bad.

—*Billie Lee Apodaca Tinoco*
Plano, Texas

Standing at the foot of the stables by the driveway, Muffy Markwart shoved the letter from *Vogue* asking her to model their new fall fashions into the pocket of her Neiman-Marcus silk and angora suit; looked up at her beautiful two-million-dollar redwood designer home that had recently been the subject of feature articles in *Town and Country*, *Better Homes and Gardens*, and *Art and Antiques*; looked at the Porsche, Ferarri, and Mercedes 560-SEL in the garage; petted her Grand Champion Doberman, Rebok, and her Grand Champion Quarter Horse, Perrier, and thought about her upcoming one-person show of paintings at the De Young Museum in San Francisco, and thought about her brilliant, romantic, liberated, and devastatingly sexy husband, Doug, recently promoted to Executive Vice-President of Megalith Computers International, and wondered where it had all begun to go wrong.

—*Katherine B. Rambo*
Foster City, California

As the sun descended behind the purple-shadowed mountains of the island, sending rosy-tipped kisses to the frolicking passengers on the cruise ship, a once beautiful, dark-haired woman, swathed in furs and dripping diamonds all over the deck, turned to her morose companion and asked, "Ferdinand, did you sign up for MediCal?"

—*Charlotte Krepismann*
Los Altos, California

On dramatizing emotions: Let your readers know when your characters are really feeling something. Find a way to dramatize emotions:

"Tears coursing down her cheeks, she hurled herself to the floor, kicking and pounding until the boards splintered. She was the one who should have been promoted to assistant general manager!"

This subtle yet effective dramatization enables the reader literally to *see* emotion.

THE WAY
WE LOVE NOW

Dialogue: With the judicious application of adverbs, anyone can write snappy dialogue:

"Don't bother me anymore!" he said testily.

"Then I won't!" she said precipitantly.

"But don't give up too easily!" he said worriedly.

"Then I won't!" she said reassuringly (and repetitively).

See how easy it is to put any words you want into your characters' mouths and then give stage directions afterward? By this simple device you have pinpoint control over your characters' tone of voice.

Her pouting eyes enslaved his, gently coaxing them toward her heaving cleavage, dappled with sweat beads which, had she been able to boast of a more affluent parentage, could have just as well been pearls on this or any other hot, dry August evening at Bucky's Burger Barn, and he knew instinctively that she was unquestionably sesame seed bun, well-done, no onions.
—*Rosalea Maher*
Omaha, Nebraska

After playing the final note of her solo, Julia haughtily tossed back her flaming auburn curls, emptied her trumpet's spit valve onto the smooth wooden floor, and sauntered proudly off the stage, unaware that Rodney, sitting in the first row of the audience, was rapturously gazing at the glistening pool of saliva she had left behind—the auditorium lights dancing off the soft, foamy bubbles like sunlight on the ocean—and yearned to wipe it up with his handkerchief and take it home, knowing that it would be the only part of her he could ever possess.
—*Julie Dean Smith*
Farmington Hills, Michigan

"Drat this blasted sinus infection!" snorted Denise as she sneezed and spewed mucus in Gregory's direction for the sixteenth time, and noting his sneer of disgust and revulsion, and realizing the evening was not going to be the romantic success she so yearned for, she extracted her legs from under the table and stormed wrathfully out of the McDonald's.
—*Shannon Walker*
Redwood City, California

Larch had been afraid of this—the morning of his first date with Jennifer Junepops, the cutest cheerleader and bravest skateboarder at Fonndeley High School—and here was his face, positively stiff with freckles.

—David Rensberger
Decatur, Georgia

"I love the way you touch me, but I hate the way you look!" she said in a petulantly erotic voice.

—Larry D. Burton
Brentwood, Tennessee

How he yearned for a truly old-fashioned girl, one who would always be on-line when he logged on; one who would treasure his input in her permanent database; one who would always respond to his dot commands; yet all the while knowing that in this new world risen from the ruins of the past after the revolt against technology, he would have to settle for one of these modern women who insisted on face-to-face communication and a "back to nature" life-style.

—Dena Leathem
Parks, Arizona

There was no occasion on which Horace Ash regretted his callow youth more than when he stared across the alley into Vera Goodbody's open window and watched her toy with a Snickers bar—stroking its length, pulling it across her flaring nostrils—before she finally seized the end in her tiny, white, perfect teeth, ripped off the wrapper, and consumed it, leaving the bar itself to melt in the summer sunshine.

—Antoinette Cook
Seattle, Washington

Florence whoosed furtively as Siegfried drew her forcefully to him, his gaping masculine nostrils pulsating proudly with the Sousa march on the stereo, chosen especially to pump up an otherwise mundane evening, while his madly roving hands sought to fan the flames of her desire and swat gnats, which were annoyed by the Sousa march, and whisper above the frantic piccolo countermelody, "Florence . . . dearest . . . you are the only woman . . . within a hundred miles."

—*Donald E. Gray*
Snellville, Georgia

Thadump, *thadump*, *thadump*, the incessant pounding of Marge's breast against his forehead was aggravating, but Lars wasn't about to complain, for this was the closest he'd ever been to a real woman.   —*Tim Burns*
Indianapolis, Indiana

More on dialogue: In seeking a model for good dialogue, think of your own conversations: you talk as much as you can get away with, let the other party take a turn while you catch your breath and think about what you are going to say next, then continue with the real business, which is expressing what you want to say. Good dialogue is really monologue with a captive audience.

Faustina felt savagely with a jealous lurch of her throbbing bosom that it simply wasn't fair that the man she lived with (and what a man, broad-shouldered, gray-eyed, and drop-dead gorgeous—not only was she attached to his body like spit to a dentist's tool but she also valued his *mind*) was her brother.

—*Ingrid Proescher*
Norwich, Connecticut

The warm wind swept in from the southern sea, embracing Tanya, the barnacle scraper, causing her to pause in her work and look across the fish-littered beach to the rotting dock and humble shack that had been her home, making her think poignantly of how she would miss all this and ponder her strange good luck at having been chosen as a mail-order bride, and, idly scratching her massive girth, wonder if her groom-to-be had correctly converted stones to pounds and if she would be happy as the first lady of America's largest city.

—*Barbara C. Kroll*
Kennett Square, Pennsylvania

She was subtle, supple, and had the right moves, and as Lonnie gazed deep, deep into her blueberry-hued eyes, he knew she would become his madness if he could not move beyond one question: What was that thing on her lip?

—*Ric Bohy*
Harper Woods, Michigan

Anne stirred the cheese soufflé furiously, wishing it were Jared's guts.

—*Cindy Clements Blewett*
Austin, Texas

As I awoke and turned to face the hideous, bloody pighead next to me in bed, and discovered beautiful Emma gone, I was forced to muse if I had been too hard on her, or if last night's party with the Harvard Club when I ordered Emma to dress as our recently sacked maid and wash everyone's feet had *really* spelled the end of our fairy-tale marriage.

—*Chris Perry*
Portland, Oregon

Oh, sure, all the superficial signs were present: the bored-to-death yawn, the inert limbs and vacant eyes, the imploring whine, "Yeah, yeah, the earth is moving for me too, but will you please hurry up—I have a dentist's appointment today," but was Deanne really tired of their sex life after three months of marriage, Jack pondered.   —*Nevin Hawkins*
Manhattan Beach, California

"He's dead!" she thought as he slumped over his soup, the tie she had given him to mark their anniversary only two weeks before trailing turmeric-tinted lentil sludge all over her nice white tablecloth.   —*Barbara Russell*
Saffron Walden, Essex, England

"He's scratching my neck again," thought Muffy desperately, "this time I must be strong," but it was too late, for Muffy's left leg—which seemed to have a mind of its own—was already making the bizarre twitching movements.

—*Michael K. Young*
Randallstown, Maryland

VILE PUNS

Myth: In the best stories, characters are dynamic and undergo some significant change by the story's end. Sometimes they will have simply grown and now are more mature, more emotionally and mentally equipped for living.

Reality: This formulation is too abstract and unsatisfying for the common reader, who would be happier just to see heroes and heroines with more power and money, something they can *use*.

Dawn crept slowly over the sparkling emerald expanse of the country club golf course, trying in vain to remember where she had dropped her car keys. —*Sally Sams*
Ben Lomond, California

Guido Marishino looked at his Thompson sub-machine gun, with its gentle spiral of smoke climbing from the once-flaming muzzle, then looked back at the crumpled, bullet-ridden body of the street performer with his blood-spattered makeup, and realized with sadness that no matter how much money they had paid him to do it, a mime was a terrible thing to waste.
—*Brian J. Bargender, Inc.*
Wausau, Wisconsin

Although Sarah had an abnormal fear of mice, it did not keep her from eeking out a living at a local pet store.
—*Richard W. O'Bryan*
Perrysburg, Ohio

"Due to your excessive consumption of egg and lemon sauces, Mr. Pigout, we must pull all your teeth and replace them with a chrome plate, but you'll soon find there's no plate like chrome for the hollandaise. —*Gloria Buckner*
Fort Wayne, Indiana

When the meteorite found and flattened Will Suckup, the peddler of Hoovers, as he walked up to Mrs. Greenblatt's front door, some people said it happened because nature abhors a vacuum-cleaner salesman. —*Manson Campbell*
Eugene, Oregon

Randi-Sue Robinson offered me more, far more, than mere money if I could find a cure for her extreme allergic reaction to fish, but as I examined her magnificently constructed upper torso, now covered with hives and bearing an uncanny resemblance to a bas-relief map of Twin Peaks, Idaho, I knew better than to make any rash promises.　　—*Bob Pollock*
Norwood, Massachusetts

"Don't you dare correct me, you pedantic wimp: I don't give a damn whether he's foundering or floundering, the man is going under the water for keeps!" she expostulated, exasperated—when, suddenly, he saw the plucky dolphin churning through the waves, his tail thrashing away a mile a minute, but it could be a fluke, he ruminated.
—*Jay Cates*
Vancouver, British Columbia, Canada

Abstract and concrete language: Some language is broad and abstract; other language is narrow and concrete. The California Peripheral Canal would have been broad and concrete.

Fredericks peered over his shoulder as he hurried nervously through the shadowy canyon of the garment district, and never saw the chintz that hurtled down from a tenth-floor window and hit him like a bolt from the blue.

—*Dan Bernstein*
Riverside, California

Open only from 7:00 P.M. until midnight, the U.S. Treasury facility at Burbank is known as the world's largest after-dinner mint.
—*John C. Wilson*
Santa Monica, California

As a scientist, Throckmorton knew that if he were ever to break wind in the sound chamber he would never hear the end of it.
—*David C. Mortensen*
Pocatello, Idaho

Bits of him would remain pieced in her memory, as it was for her he wore the ring which snagged, launching him through the limb-shredder.
—*Greg E. Bisel*
Fresno, California

It seemed the fall didn't last too long this year, Betty lamented as she gazed up at the bare old oak tree before brushing herself off and checking for bruises.
—*James Edward Williams*
Columbus, Ohio

The Pope claimed it was indeed the remains of that symbol of Christianity on which the Lord had died so that the sins of mankind could be forgiven them, but the attorney for the state doubted it would stand up to his cross-examination.
—*Janet M. Kaul*
Redwood City, California

Jimmy was a very smart boy, and he enjoyed church very much, but when the choir began singing "Gladly the Cross I'd Bear," he didn't concentrate on singing the song as he should have; instead, he wondered why Gladly didn't go to an ophthalmologist and why they were singing a song in church about a woodland animal with an eye problem anyway.

—*Timothy House*
Palmdale, California

"Calm down, son; I can see that you're upset and injured, but I've got to tell you the truth—there's a psychic force turning men into various were-beasts in the fields surrounding this farm (more potent than I can even guess, so I'm not going to try), controlling our movements; so when you tried to leave, well, you were attacked by a bull-were, Lytton!"

—*Jeanne Leiter*
Arcadia, California

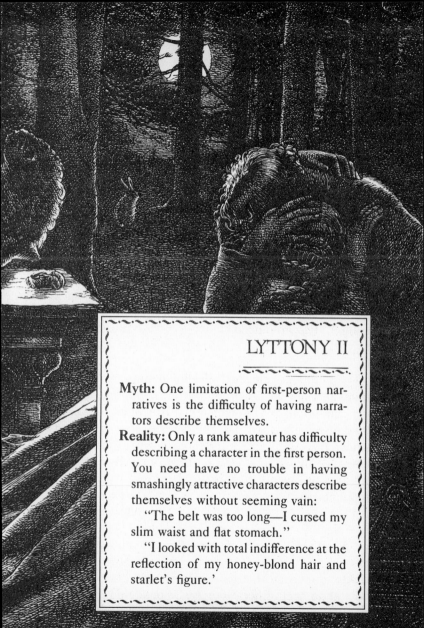

LYTTONY II

Myth: One limitation of first-person narratives is the difficulty of having narrators describe themselves.

Reality: Only a rank amateur has difficulty describing a character in the first person. You need have no trouble in having smashingly attractive characters describe themselves without seeming vain:

"The belt was too long—I cursed my slim waist and flat stomach."

"I looked with total indifference at the reflection of my honey-blond hair and starlet's figure.'

Edmond waited, then, immediately, waited again.

—*Donald Smyth*
Cocoa, Florida

With one last glance toward the kitchen window where Buster the budgie still flapped hysterically in his cage, Jennie Callaghan jockeyed the protesting Peterbilt out of the farmyard and up the potholed road toward the melon groves, every bone in her forty-year-old body screaming that something was wrong.

—*Anna McDougald*
Winnipeg, Manitoba, Canada

In the Mexican town of Texicallo sits a fat woman at her door staring moodily at the chickens; it is she who best of all recalls Enrico Prumbello.

—*Y. David Shulman*
Brooklyn, New York

Tired of being called a "sniveling popinjay," Winslow Forbush stuck his jaw out at himself in the mirror, clenched his fists, and intoned, "I'm gonna make them all pay, or I guess some of them at least, but they're gonna stand up and take notice, for sure!" and it all came down to just one thing, murder—murder, or at least hurting somebody badly, but not badly enough to initiate a lawsuit, because lawyers were rather frightening to Winston.

—*Michael J. Melen*
Baltimore, Maryland

"Damn Geoffrey and his exotic pets!" muttered Millicent, crushing out her cigarette on the still-writhing body of Bullwinkle, the Giant Madagascar Hissing Cockroach impaled on the stiletto heel of her shoe, as she pondered again how she had jilted the brilliant, if somewhat palsied, brain surgeon and

laser researcher, Mortimer Dinglehopper, and married a hand-some, wealthy, and virile eccentric multibillionaire with a pen-chant for odd livestock and a strict old-fashioned belief that marriage was meant to last a lifetime. —*P. A. Carty*
Clive, Iowa

In the Beginning there was God . . . but after a while there was unrest in the Garden of Eden and then some more time passed and Local #107 in Pottsborough, Massachusetts, went out on a wildcat strike on July 3, 1953 (but I'm getting ahead of my story). —*K. C. Kelly-Chaulk*
South Pasadena, California

Yud's spear and club still glistened with the blood of the antelope now skinned by his brother Glop and ready for the fire being prepared by Glop's mate, Fin, who caught Yud's perilously close-set eyes with leaping heart; and as Yud's gaze caressed the sun-scorched droop of Fin's breast they both knew, simultaneously, in that unforgettable moment, with the jiving flames revealing the bat-infested crevices of their little granite cavern, that they were the very first couple on Earth to fall in love. —*Gina Williams*
Gwynedd, Wales

"*Mein Gott im Himmel*," murmured Der Führer, "I was com-manding the immediate presence of Goebbels, not gerbils!" as he waded through the now chest-high throng of rodents, his purposeful pin-point pupils quickly regaining their cus-tomary expression of almost saintly Teutonic benevolence.
—*Andy Otes*
Sydney, Australia

As her fragile, aging hands fondled the rotting tomato, she reminisced of harvests past—there was no tomorrow, only today and sweet memories of those golden days, the sky an azure bowl, the sun a shining orb, and stretching endlessly the fields of green, dotted by crimson globes, and stoop, pick, stoop, pick, stoop, pick.   *—J. M. Jamison*
San Francisco, California

The horror!—ah, the horror!—of it all envelops me e'en now in the gelid amnion from which no natural force may e'er propel me, claw me, drag me forth, so enervating was that unholy power which laid its claim to my very soul and to all things of the earth my outer husk might touch; so puissantly vile it was that to permit the most halting syllable of this unspeakable profanation to pass my lips would blight the auditor and drag him down to utter ruin; so instead I'll tell you my favorite story about Bunnykins and Meemo.
  —Cecily Korell
Arcadia, California

On accepting criticism: There is a major difference between the way that an amateur and a professional accept criticism. An amateur takes the criticism to heart and suffers a severe crisis in confidence; the professional recognizes it as a product of envy and incomprehension.

Young Goldblax, like his father before him, wondered if he'd made the right decision by entering manhood, and now

for the thousandth time today—ever since the drying rawhide strips began cutting deep into his wrists, inexorably pulling his arms in opposite directions—he wished he'd opted for the more traditional Bar Mitzvah instead. —*David La Vere*
Dallas, Texas

"How ya doin?" chortled Priscilla Bodkin to her aerobics class, little realizing that in thirty-six hours she would be a love slave in a Moroccan dungeon. —*Jeffrey Agrell*
Lucerne, Switzerland

Well, anyway, by golly, Beauregard P. Befudilus sat his horse, without a saddle even, just like a professional horsesitter and, as a result, was much in demand, whenever southern gentlemen took long, lazy, leisure-filled jaunts to exotic places like Placerville and Pleasant Acres, as a horsesitter, since he never hardly ever in no way objected to sitting horses, even if he had to do it without a saddle and on short notice over the weekends without extra pay and with expenses coming out of his own pocket and with crabby horses and even crabbier clients. —*Robert Lawson*
Monroe, Washington

In reflecting on his sexual life, Jackson recalled with some piquancy his first wife, the talented linguist whose enthusiastic and unabandoned practice of glottals and palatals, voice and unvoiced vowels, prurient plosives and decadent diphthongs, had caused him to writhe like some crazy tilde over a suggestive Spanish verb, but who left him ultimately for a pidgin specialist she met at an Esperanto conference—the last message she recorded on the answering machine, as if to mock him, having been in her new lover's specialty: "Me bilong wayaway. Haka u, haka me, allasame no."

—*Gary M. Cole*
Berkeley, California

As Dirk stood at the open window through which the Ninja warriors had entered, staring at his brother-in-law's unconscious antelope, which was bleeding on the new mauve wall-to-wall shag carpet, he was suddenly beset by an overwhelming sense of *déjà vu*.

—*Tracy G. Stampfli*
Bloomington, Indiana

He was the best of mimes, he was the worst of mimes, he was the page of wisdom, he was the page of foolishness, he was the embodiment of belief, he was the embodiment of incredulity, he was the liaison of Light, he was the liaison of Darkness, he was the rise of despair, he was the fall of hope, he was everything, he was nothing, he was going toward limbo, he was going to purgatory in a hand basket, he was—in short— a mime.

—*L. B. Brumage*
Elizabeth, New Jersey

ROMANCE: HISTORICAL, GOTHICAL, AND GENERICAL

On writing romances: There are certain benefits to working with generic romances, which usually run to about only 50,000 words. You should be able to write one of these in about half the time it would take you to write another novel twice as long.

The sun fought like a tiger to escape from its cage of dark clouds and finally emerged gently as a lamb, bestowing its soft warmth upon Liane, her golden hair blown by the wind which swept across the high rocky hill overlooking her ancestral home that was once threatened by fire and flood but was now owned by the man who killed her father, raped her grandmother, and was soon to become her husband.

—*Helen Niemeyer*
Downers Grove, Illinois

In the wan light of the Biloxi dawn, Cytheraea lay crumpled on the trundle bed like so much used Kleenex, or perhaps like the sticky remnants of a box of Cap'n Crunch cereal that someone has dumped out, callously and without any regard for their mother's feelings after cleaning the kitchen, in order to get to the free prize inside, her honor.

—*Charles Dodt*
Concord, California

Claudette Marie Françoise de la Montagne du Champ en Ville gazed petulantly out of the window of Château de Champignon, and as she caressed her exquisite petites *bottines* and the *peau de soie* of her lovely dress, as she looked out again at Village en Vallee far below, her expression at once *triste* and *charmante*, she could think only of her lost *amour*, Elmer Lunt, a high school chemistry teacher from Cleveland, Ohio.

—*Mairin Dudley*
Elizabeth Wissinger
Pacific Palisades, California

"Oh, what good is the elegance and wealth to which I have been born when the only man I love, Baron Phillipe de Blanqueville, loves another; what good is beauty and a heart that throbs beneath my ample breast when the blood in his veins courses for *her;* what good is this splendid but tasteful marble fireplace before me when the fire in his heart is not mine to tend?" the Countess Maressa, a handsome woman even at the age of thirty-four, cried inquisitively as she flung herself on the pink velvet settee.   —*Veronica Fowler*
Ames, Iowa

"Purposefully!" was Trask's gutturally terse half-reply, spoken only after a pause sufficient in duration for his date's gaze to lift curiously from the sand caked on the nearly lifeless cetacean's body to the birthmarked side of his face, lowered now to protect from the wave-whipped ocean wind those deeply Humperdinckian eyes, which he had trained impassively on the jagged-edged and salt-encrusted nail of his big toe, as it traced silvery quarter-moons on the skin just below the animal's blowhole.   —*Jon Thompson*
Cupertino, California

Callously, with no thought for the morning—or, for that matter, for the endless mornings cascading down the years like the water from the falls which vortexed the Hudson and Mohawk rivers near Cohoes, that city of crass commercialism and culture, rather like the dichotomous rivers, swirling together with waters from north, south, east, and west, Kort Leadbetter touched her warm, pulsating knee.   —*Jean Bourgeois*
Scotia, New York

> **On settings in generic romantic novels:** Settings should be contemporary but exotic; a romantic setting is worthy of a romantic story:
>
> "Many outsiders didn't know it," mused Clio, "but summers in Boise were so hot and dry that the locals often gave up entirely on sprinklers and resorted to flooding their lawns."
>
> Later you can have the hero and heroine splash toward one another right through a submerged lawn, a clever and poetic variation on the lovers running toward one another in slow motion across an open field, though Boise has lots of those, too.

"No! No! A thousand times no!" poor Penelope squealed as her pixyish frame disappeared beneath the lust-engorged loins of Hector the hulk, mindful all the while that she still had 997 "no's" to go. *—Brian D. Smith*
         Indianapolis, Indiana

At midnight Mona moaned and let her mink slide malcontentedly to the marble floor as she stood mesmerized, trying mainly to imagine that Miguel was more, much more, than the miserable mouse of a man she knew him to be, so much more than the miserly and mundane, malapropical and milquetoastish, maladapted and slightly mutated masculine mimicry of something that starts with "M." *—Richard Allen Hughes*
         Excelsior, Minnesota

The bloody kangaroos had been unusually jumpy for the past few days, what with the eucalyptus reeking so of Vicks Vaporub, and now this grossly ruddy dried-out morning was upon the outback, and Barry knew that Sheila would wait no more, wait no more for him to gouge from the sullen earth of Coober Pedy the humungous opals of down under; knew, too, that she would announce that her waiting was at an end by going walkabout—and taking his pet koala with her.

> —*Ruth Paya*
> *Menlo Park, California*

She knew she had seen those delts before, and the pecs—had, in truth, done more than gaze at them—but it was only when his blue Jockey shorts dropped to the throw rug that she again smelled the frangipani-scented air and felt in her veins the pounding of the surf that had shaken their tiny, moonlight-flooded cabin on that night of abandon in Pago Pago.

> —*David H. Green*
> *Great Falls, Virginia*

Gently lifting Gerrard's well-manicured hand from where it had been idly snapping the elastic of her black lace panties, Arabella led him to the trellised terrace where they could see dawn's fuchsia tentacles snatching the last twinkling stars from the night sky and glinting rosily off Gerrard's monocle as Arabella whispered breathily, "All of Gerontalia depends on us, all those future generations breaking their shackles and following behind; whatever the consequences, my dearest, tonight I must dance as I have never danced before."

> —*Barbara W. Bassett*
> *Carson City, Nevada*

The gale-force wind billowed her long gingham skirt and shoulder-length raven-black hair, and the spray from the raging sea, as it broke on the jagged rocks below, chilled her bare throat and arms and brought tears to her emerald-green eyes, and Simone realized that her escape from the evil Baron Grenfell, with his dark, brooding eyes, bony, grasping hands, and maniacal laugh, was for naught because she would now have to return to Moormire Manor, with its dusty, shadowy halls that echoed with the footsteps of the ghosts of past generations, to ask him for an aspirin for the cold she was catching here at the cliff's edge.
—*Gail Eileen Gaddy*
San Diego, California

Romantic endings: Readers of romances insist on upbeat endings:

"As Dexter enfolded her in his powerful yet gentle arms, she understood at last the meaning of life: nothing really hurts, the bad stuff happens only to other people, and you get everything you want."

This should satisfy the reader too sophisticated or cynical to accept "and they lived happily ever after."

SUDDEN TURNS

On poetic justice: Readers like it when unsympathetic characters come to a fitting end:

"Miles had died as he had lived. Someone had slipped a golf club through the waist of his drawstring pants and spun it like a propeller. The effect reduced Miles to a pair of giant purple bratwursts."

The scruffily dressed motorcycle gang pulled Lori's white Corvette over to the side of the deserted country road and hurriedly began to rotate her tires. —*Gerald W. Shigley*
Machesney Park, Illinois

Ted always hated crowds, and the noisy, cheerful one at his execution was no exception. —*Paul Alan Chase*
Carson, California

Something about her reminded me of Paris—perhaps the intoxicating redolence of her Chanel No. 5, or the sleek, exquisite lines of her Oscar de la Renta original, or the scale model of the Eiffel Tower that was strapped to her shoulder.
—*Kenneth C. Cundy*
Berkeley, California

There was about him a certain *air*, a hint of *élan*, a touch of *gentillesse*, a *soupçon* of *je ne sais quoi* that set him apart from the other Harley Davidson bikers. —*Bruce Pearson*
Midland, Texas

"Soup's on!" she shouted from the galley, preening in the secret knowledge that none of those gross characters whose appetites she had just alerted would ever guess she was speaking French.
—*Maynard Mack*
New Haven, Connecticut

"Is it too late to take back what I said to the jury?" I asked the priest as we walked down the narrow hallway.
—*Evelyn Villegas*
Cypress, California

As the Civil War dragged on on its weary course, matriarchal Clarabelle Beauregard continued to upbraid her handsome son Ravenal because of the lack of money with which to purchase the frills and furbelows so dear to her selfish heart, not caring a fig that all the help had fled the plantation and there was no one to bring in the cotton, when at last her son had had enough, seizing his whining parent by the hand, dragged her to the spacious balcony which overlooked the empty fields and with a sweeping wave of his hand which embraced all his ancestral acres, he cried in exasperation: "Look, Ma! No hands!"

—*Stafford C. Gillespie*
London, Ontario, Canada

She was conscious of the kisses, of her racing pulse and swimming head, of his hands, but most of all, the ecstasy as she lay with him, and he with her, their bodies pressed together as he did his will—her will—and left everything to a second cousin in Sheboygan.   —*John E. Farrow*
Albuquerque, New Mexico

That had always been my dream: to soar, raptor-like, trailing invisible contrails of silent air like the first pale fingers of dawn behind me, and drift like down, nay, like the merest gossamer, on the endless horizon of pristine space, clouds spread below like fairy castles of cottage cheese and flavored yogurt, and diamond-studded Night above; but my eyes weren't good enough so they made me a cook instead.

—*Ray C. Gainey*
Indianapolis, Indiana

The dashingly elegant, gray-haired airline pilot, smart and immaculate in his freshly pressed uniform, slammed the door

of his brand-new cherry-red Ferrari and skipped to the front door of his dream home—a refrigerator box under the Washington Avenue Bridge. —*Sheila J. Brooks*
Apple Valley, Minnesota

Retiring after thirty-five years as a chalkboard salesman, Walter looked on with pride at his collection of basketball trophies that he had stolen from high schools from all across the country. —*Lee P. Bailey*
Mississippi State, Mississippi

I shot up out of bed with the first blood-curdling shriek—the beginning of the now regular series of hair-whitening, skin-crawling, nerve-shattering, banshee-like howls which chilled the deepest recesses of my soul and echoed through the haunted corridors of my once-serene home every night, at three o'clock sharp, for the past two weeks—ah, but soon my house would be exorcised and calm restored, since my sis was returning from Europe tomorrow and taking my little nephew back. —*Clark Ochikubo*
Stanford, California

The full moon broke through the scudding black clouds and, as its cold light threw the bleak facades of the tombstones into sharp relief, it revealed the presence of the great slavering mastiff at the open door of the crypt, its satanic red eyes glittering as it slowly raised its massive head skyward and wagged its little tail. —*Brian J. Collins*
Ottawa, Ontario, Canada

On **characterization:** Your characters do not have to emerge immediately as fully developed characters. As the story moves along, they will have time to flesh out. At the beginning of *Charlotte's Web*, for example, Wilbur probably does not weigh much more than two and a half pounds.

As the sun sank slowly in the west, so did Penelope as she soaked up those last remaining rays from her towel hastily thrown over some quicksand.   —*Stephen D. Bock*
Marietta, Georgia

CLERICAL ERRORS

Myth: Good books are not written; they are rewritten.

Reality: This is conventional advice of professionals to amateurs, of people on the gravy train to those who want to board. If you fall for this one, you will natter away on a book you have already written in more time than it will take you to write another.

The vibrassae on her pet's snout stood uniquely erect as Sister Mary Ignatius unceremoniously removed her vestments and absentmindedly stroked the cat's fur in a vicarious counterclockwise fashion while contemplating breaking her holy vows of obedience and acquiescing to the theatric act of self-immolation on Passover at the Smithsonian Mall to protest the archdiocese's abridgement of her academic freedom to teach a course on feline worship at the convent, knowing full well that such an emancipating act of self-expression would immediately trigger an IRS audit.

—*Stanley M. Bierman, M.D.*
Los Angeles, California

Sister Mary "The Reverent Rambler" Ignatius crashed to the turf and ate dirt under the crush of bodies, her bones creaking as she squirmed out from under the groaned mass; yes, she hurt, she hurt like h——l, but pain was nothing next to the cheering of the crowd as she took her place in the backfield in the fullback slot, the spearhead of the convent's wishbone attack.

—*Mark Diller*
Eugene, Oregon

"Dank, dank, dank—this convent is too damn dank!" screamed the Mother Superior, stamping her foot so hard that her rosary broke and hailed Hail Marys like balls in a Pachinko machine (a Japanese gambling device with automatic payoff) onto the floor until one came to rest under her heel, causing her to slip on her fanny and add one more Mary (for that was her name) to the pile.

—*Dr. Billy V. Koen*
Austin, Texas

Sister Clare folded the dispensation and tapped it thoughtfully against her teeth as she gazed out over the Norfolk Broads: should she leave the Order and marry the last male heir of the ancient De La Strange family, witless though he was, or should she take on Mother Maria's latest assignment, that of teaching the fine art of paper cutting to the girls of the Blue Class, who even now clamored around her, their eyes puzzled, their scissors creating maimed nasturtiums, unearthly laburnums, and failed geraniums which matted together and drifted about like sticky new cut grass all over Sister Martha's formerly immaculate floor?

—*Margaret J. Mason*
San Francisco, California

The arrival of Sister Debbie's beau, occurring as it did during Father Noster's phlegmatic rendition of benediction, unnerved Mother Puleze so much she thwacked Novice Scotia with her rosary crucifix, even though she had done nothing wrong—yet.

—*Fender Tucker*
Las Cruces, New Mexico

As the priest sipped the alum-tainted sacramental wine, his lips and entire mouth puckered relentlessly until he resembled a Chow about-face, and he wondered, not for the first time, if Sister Mary Incognito was taking her religious duties seriously.

—*Jennifer C. Kemner*
Grandview, Missouri

"You take the apple, Adam, girls prefer boas!" Eve said, wrapping it snuggly around her neck.

—*Barbara C. Kroll*
Kennett Square, Pennsylvania

"As you are aware," said the Bishop, "I have encouraged responsible liturgical innovation in this diocese; but I am at a loss to follow, let alone approve, your intended theological meaning with 'The Lord is my doggy bag.' "

—Timothy Poston
Venice, California

Cardinal Pinnipiedi, Keeper of the Seals at the Vatican, desperately tried to stir up the fire in his grate, feeding it with slightly damp old manuscripts, which sent up a plume of white smoke from his chimney and made the crowd gathered outside think a new Pope had been elected, when in fact he was trying to revive a recently orphaned seal pup which was lying, cold and shivering, on the red-satin covers of his ornate four-poster bed.

—Alec Kitroeff
Psychico, Greece

Getting published: Getting into print is simply a matter of knowing your market. At *Redbook* magazine, for example, they get about 36,000 short story submissions a year, but they publish only fifty. Simple math tells you that you should be able to crack this market by submitting 720 short stories annually.

The night after Bishop Denton, woozy from an overdose of snuff, slipped off the balcony of the Very Friendly Arms Inn and fell into Marsden Lake, his body marred beyond recognition by a vindictive flounder, the slim yet not unbuxom Miss

Havashaw was taking a brass rubbing of her recently departed identical twin sister when the Reverend Gump hobbled across the nave of the ancient church, his wooden leg pounding against the worn stone floor, and with a note of irritation in his deep, resonant voice said, "Rubbing her will never bring her back, Iona."

—*Craig Ullman*
Medford, New York

Sister Immaculata judiciously dabbed at the droplets of blood as they fell upon her generous slice of thick-cut prime rib, being careful to use only the tip of her silk brocaded diocesan napkin, at the same time struggling in vain to conceal her quickly manifesting stigmata while overhead droned the heavy brogue of Monsignor Quinncannon extolling her many virtues, she being the guest of honor, making her feel chastened and unsaintly for being unable to control the rising disgust she felt over bleeding upon a one-hundred-dollar-plate "Holy Names Sister of the Year" dinner, yet she was determined to be strengthened by the fact that God had guided her hand in deviating from her first choice: Dover Sole in a *Beurre Blanc* sauce.

—*T. W. Avolio-Toly*
Portland, Oregon

"If I had only remembered what my mother told me at the supper table about religion and politics," thought Simon Peter, "I wouldn't be running from the Romans now!"

—*Timothy Poston*
Venice, California

In the tenth year following God's creation of the Heavens and Earth, the Heavenly Hosts hosted a surprise anniversary celebration for Him—a Galactic Gala MC'd by the Man with the Golden Lips, Gabriel Gillespie (whose famous descendant, begat many generations thereafter, would also play the trumpet and would be known as Dizzy)—and it featured the Paradise at Night Players in a toe-tapping musical salute to history entitled, "Decade I—The Formative Years"; but the highlight of the evening had been a surprise visit from the Prince of Darkness Himself, who had the cloud crowd roaring with his fiery roast of The Omnipotent One; when suddenly the ceremony was interrupted by a Messianic Mesenger with an urgent note for God that said Adam and Eve's babysitter was on the phone with news that something very strange was happening in the Garden and they should all come at once!

—*K. C. Kelly-Chaulk*
South Pasadena, California

Themes in children's stories: Authorities have noted that many fairy and folk tales aimed at children have a retributive pattern, meaning that kids can really identify with getting even, especially when the victims are authority figures or more powerful and privileged peers. In others words, children love to see the strong and prosperous brought down, though we adults have long outgrown such impulses.

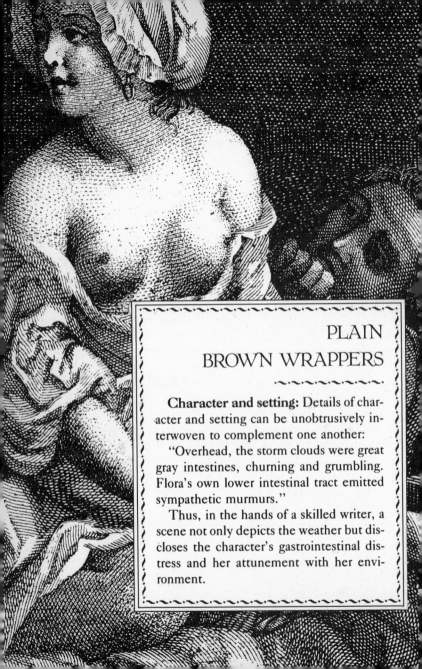

PLAIN
BROWN WRAPPERS

Character and setting: Details of character and setting can be unobtrusively interwoven to complement one another:

"Overhead, the storm clouds were great gray intestines, churning and grumbling. Flora's own lower intestinal tract emitted sympathetic murmurs."

Thus, in the hands of a skilled writer, a scene not only depicts the weather but discloses the character's gastrointestinal distress and her attunement with her environment.

As she lay there dozing next to me, one voice inside my head kept saying, "Relax . . . you're not the first doctor who's ever slept with one of his patients," but another kept reminding me, "Howard, you're a veterinarian."

—*Dick Wilson*
Orlando, Florida

Folding up and putting down *Moby Dick* in the stained seat beside her in the front row, the braless redhead in the diaphanous miniskirt crossed her sleek legs, threw back her head, cleared her throat, raised her beringed left hand to stop the sophomoric lecture, and demanded in a gravelly voice that the priapismic prof who had been leering at her since September explain to them how Van Leeuwenhoek came by the semen sample he scrupulously studied under the screwbarrel microscope.

—*David L. Hoof*
Germantown, Maryland

Dr. Ruth Weisenheimer, Sex Therapist to the Stars, threw up her hands as well as her breakfast (orange juice, Froot-Loops, and black coffee, apparently) when I revealed my fascination with TV weather girl Kathy Quinlan's great set of isobars, and explained the scheme I had concocted to simultaneously raise her temperature and her relative humidity.

—*Bob Pollock*
Norwood, Massachusetts

He had made her come again and again, night after night, against her will until she almost thought she couldn't—no—shouldn't fight it anymore, when some last hidden reserve of strength reared up on its hind legs and she broke away from

his demanding grasp, resolving never to see *Casablanca* at a retrospective theater again.   —*Kathy Toy*
Toronto, Ontario, Canada

Myra Doodlewick, professional substitute teacher for more than fifty years, strode over to Jimmy Strannly and raised her stainless steel, razor-sharp yardstick over her head with a two-fisted grip that prompted the appearance of twenty steaming, amber puddles beneath the sticky, corduroyed-clad seats of the terrified children.   —*Barbara Daley Robidoux*
Candia, New Hampshire

On writing for juveniles: You can't catch up your juvenile readers too quickly. After three sentences, a JR (juvenile reader) begins to wonder, "What's in this for me?" Give the little beggar a reason to keep reading:

"The first page of this novel has been soaked in a poisonous solution, and you must keep reading to find the antidote. Otherwise, it will be two weeks before it will be safe for you to touch yourself."

"Classical conditioning strikes again," drawled anthropologist John Bell as he noted the stirring in his loins at the sight of the native women with the fifteen-inch lip discs and recollected senior prom night when his date, Miss Vicki, split with his best friend and he was left with nothing but his imagination and a dog-earred copy of *National Geographic*.

—*Mary L. Billingsley*
Shawnee, Kansas

Trigonometry, that graceful limb of the queenly branch of the Tree of Knowledge, which mirrored, with its sinusoidal pulsating and rhythmic continuousness, with its interpreting and interminable sensuousness, with its relentless up and down throbbing of its maxima and minima and its perfect points of inflection—her own young, budding, and perfecting form— had always been Tammi's favorite turn-on.

—*Donald R. Dewitt*
Fairbanks, Alaska

Often, as old Jake suffered chapped lips during them harsh mountain winters, why, just to keep from licking them, ever' morning he got hisself up and lifted his pack-mule's tail and kissed the surprised animal's bowhind, but it never worked, and he always spit when he talked.   —*James Russell Davis*
Sunnyvale, California

"Stop!" shrieked Beulah as her would-be attacker, his foul breath an unforgivable blot on the otherwise clean night air, fumbled clumsily with greasy fingers at her bodice, where her more-than-ample bosom strained against the thin silk, the milky-white globes threatening with every gasping breath to break free and soar uninhibitedly into the sunset.

—*Carolyn Huston*
Monterey, California

We thought we were being discreet, writhing and moaning on the dining room floor, my legs wrapped around his neck in an ecstatic frenzy of pit-bull-like desire, until Father Flannagan looked up from his liverwurst sandwich and remarked, "That'll cost you three extra Hail Marys!"

—*Elizabeth Anderson*
Lansing, Illinois

The swinging, singing Kremmler Sisters—Patti, Maxine, and Delight—hair shining in cascades of loveliness, barely contained in vibrant disk-festooned snoods, hips swirling in almost disastrously tight khaki skirts, bubble breasts straining to escape from demure sweetheart necklines, opened the show to near pandemonium as nearly 3,000 achingly horny sailors yelled, whistled, catcalled, stamped, and even clapped their release.

—*Donald C. Cameron*
South Laguna, California

Failing to notice the turquoise eelskin dangling jauntily from his trouser front, I did not at first grasp Enoch's immense charms, but then I am forever unmindful of the subtle stratagems by which men perpetually advertise rank within their peculiar pecking order.

—*Larry Bennett*
Chicago, Illinois

RIDERS OF THE MAUVE SAGE

Describing the unfamiliar: You can describe even experiences that are remote from your own observation if you do it with conviction. Simply draw upon the experience you *do* have. Suppose you grew up in the city with only a dog for a pet but you need to write about horses:

"The pony sat back on its haunches, scratched an ear with its hind leg, and tried to remember where he had buried his oats."

Nothing infuriated Harriet Beechley more than when some-one shot her brother Roger out of the saddle from a hiding place behind a big rock.
—B. Jack Gebhardt
Fort Collins, Colorado

Buckeye Bellbouche never knew if it was the sudden crack of the bounty hunter's knuckle, or just the way his six-gun cast a rainbow in the hot sunlight of Fried Chicken Gulch, but he realized later that it was sheer instinct that made him dive off his cayuse into the wash, roll through the untumbled tumbleweeds, slide over the week-old remains of a forgotten Cherokee brunch, spin like a frontier dreidel, raise his peace-maker, and shoot enough holes in the gunman's green felt shirt to make him pass for the ugliest pool table in Arizona.
—Tim Marlowe
Arcadia, California

No one crossed the Rio Sangria and rode alone through the maze of mesas which meant death (or bad confusion) to all except an experienced tracker like Hangnails Coty, who now— canny scout that he was—tweezed a hair from his nose and held it up to see which way the wind was blowing.
—Enid Shomer
Gainesville, Florida

Howling Wolf's hawklike eyes narrowed as they beheld the column of U.S. Cavalry. "Very soon, boys in blue," he hissed, "you will wear the ceremonial red of a Comanche victim!"
—William Minors
Mississauga, Ontario, Canada

The wind whistled, the tumbleweeds tumbled, and the horses muttered their mutual assent as Big Jim MacPherson tied his mount Gunshy to the hitching post outside the Crossfile Canyon Saloon and Mesquite Grill, and burst through the gap-slatted swinging doors—the dust of the trail trailing him—ordering to the saloonkeep in a too-loud voice, "I'll have an ice-cold Perrier with a twist of kiwi!" as the dust—rising glitteringly in the fading twilight, its gossamer weight dragging it back down—underscored the extent of Big Jim's social gaffe.

—*Greg Martinez*
Gainesville, Florida

Ordinary men, broken and ravaged by the scouring prairie winds, would have looked through sand-stung eyes at the bleak dead sea of dry grass across the Nebrasky landscape and given up, and Ned Bimpler was one of these men.

—*Wanda E. Seamster*
Anchorage, Alaska

"Go fer yer kicker, ya no-good son of a pig-thief!" snarled the menacing, black-hatted, barrel-chested, one-eyed stranger as I stepped offa ma trail-worn, fly-swattin', two-hundred-dollar-saddle-covered faithful gray mare and prepared to head into Jake Barnes's Last-Chance-of-a-Meal-and-Beer-Before-2,000-Miles-o'-Desert Saloon in Silver City on the north edge of the High Lonesome country that early summer day just before sundown.

—*Tom Maxwell*
Van Nuys, California

Little Prairie Chicken plied his oar along the rapids, for soon he would be at the white man's trading post, where he would have to speak sententiously in constipated sentences

with hacked syntax, although for now he was at peace with the Great Spirit and trying madly not to spill into the rushing, rock-strewn water.   —*Mary Lee Ward*
                                              Chicago, Illinois

"But aren't we treating the noble Redman wrong when we steal his land, slaughter his buffalo, and trample on his sacred burial grounds!" Donohue cried impassionedly and was quite beginning to get on Sergeant Thork's nerves when a Paiute arrow mercifully entered the young trooper's left ear and put a pointed end to his diatribe.   —*David Willingham*
                                        Georgetown, Tennessee

As the two lonely figures—one tall and slim and astride a prancing, golden palomino, the other shorter, rounder, and perched on a plodding, sleepy gray burro—circled the huge, flaming red sandstone monolith, their eyes met a random jumble of windswept, broken-down shacks that seemed to have been tossed across the desert like so many dirty dice: Laramie.
                                          —*Bruce Brakeman*
                                            Medina, Ohio

Astride his palomino, a slender-legged horse of a cream color with flaxen mane and tail, from ancestry largely of Arabian stock, Hank loosened his lariat, preparing to lasso the straying Hereford, red with a white face and markings, one of a breed of hardy beef cattle originating in Herefordshire, England.
                                          —*Jean McCluskey*
                                          Laguna Hills, California

Jake of Galilee had ridden hard from Shiloh to reach Gomorrah by sundown, and now, tying up his camel and dusting

the desert from his robes, he boldly strolled into the Lucky Leper Bar, wondering if the lovely, salacious Jessie Belle, a woman he knew a lot in his past, realized she was only a stone's throw away from destiny.
(from *High Plains Prophet*—a Biblical Western)

—*Wanda E. Seamster*
Anchorage, Alaska

Muddy gray-brown clouds scudded sporadically across the hot and steadily darkening west Texas sky as the Mule Shoe Kid scratched his scraggly beard, spat acrid brown tobacco juice onto the blazing campfire, and cursed his continued bad luck because he'd had to kill yet another unexpected visitor in the guise of a diamond-back sidewinder with his pearl-handled .45, the concussion and shock of which was enough to cause his delicate ham-and-spinach soufflé to fall for the third night in a row.

—*Laura R. Virgil*
Dallas, Texas

The roan pitched and yawed like a dinghy in a typhoon, while Stacy, with the determination of a tugboat going upriver, clung to its back like a barnacle on a schooner; to no avail, however, for the horse pitched, Stacy yawed and hit the hoof-churned-clay-and-horse-dung corral floor like a square-rigger hitting a reef in the fog, which made her bones rattle like doubloons in a pirate's chest, and caused her to swear like a stevedore.

—*Elsa Rash*
Bismarck, North Dakota

With the ends of her own long hair, black as her French silk corset, Cinnamon Rositl lashed the raging stallion surging between her thighs, naked above the fancy lace stockings she

danced in at Mary Margaret's Border Saloon, and vowed to her ancestral Aztec gods that she would recover her people's sacred trust, the golden Virgin's Torque she'd kept hidden for so long behind the bar at Mary Margaret's, the one that just this night the cowboy whose dust she now followed in the moonlight had spied and stuffed down his buckskins.
(from *Because Real Cowboys Don't Wear Underwear*)

—*Birdie Hawkins*
Aurora, Indiana

Dave spit the dry trail dust from his lips, snorted the raw burnt-flesh stink of fresh branding from his running nose, used his hands to wipe some of the greasy gelding sweat from his frayed chaps, and thought of his gal back in Topeka, Kate, with her cerulean pigmentary lining of the ciliary processes, the abundant auricular growth from the follicular involutions of the occipitofrontalis epidermal tissues, and the statuesque symmetry of her zygomatic arches.

—*William J. O'Connell*
Worcester, Massachusetts

It was a warm and overly bright day when Chad Cahill rode back into Harperville that morning (Lucy Meadows was watching fearfully from behind mauve lace curtains that exactly matched the violet color of her eyes), and as he moved slowly down the dusty main street, many pairs of eyes watched Chad's cautious progress, when suddenly there exploded a voice from behind him:

"Cut . . . now let's try this scene with a *real* horsy, Chad, instead of that damn broomstick!"

—*K. C. Kelly-Chaulk*
South Pasadena, California

On scenic description: You don't need an esoteric vocabulary to present picturesque or exotic scenes. An apt description will often serve better than precise taxonomy:

"Buck Nuggets knew the desert well—the merciless sun, the red-tailed hawks circling overhead, the shimmering horizon, the green plants all covered with poky things."

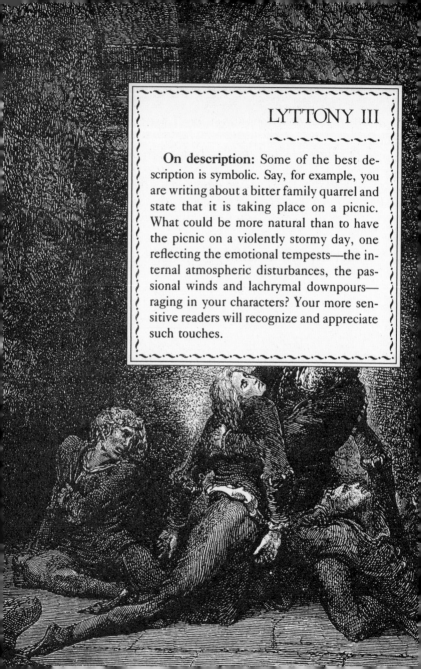

LYTTONY III

On description: Some of the best description is symbolic. Say, for example, you are writing about a bitter family quarrel and state that it is taking place on a picnic. What could be more natural than to have the picnic on a violently stormy day, one reflecting the emotional tempests—the internal atmospheric disturbances, the passional winds and lachrymal downpours—raging in your characters? Your more sensitive readers will recognize and appreciate such touches.

A horrified Jake Laird realized that an army of Sumatran giant tent caterpillars was weaving a cocoon around him, and as the process continued he began to wonder, "Will I metamorphose into a beautiful butterfly, or am I to be future food for these critters?" but then, just as the cocooning shut out the last rays of sunshine, he became drowsy and said to himself, "Heck, this isn't so bad—it's comfy-cozy in here, and besides this is one place the IRS will never think to look for me!"
—*Vern Orr*
San Pablo, California

Standing before his mirror, Napoleon thought: "*Merci*, I am short—well, not so much as diminutive, or even stunted, perhaps 'tiny' is the better word—certainly not teeny, or teenyweeny, or eentsy-weentsy—'slight' maybe, a minikin, nanoid, and elfin—should I let it be known that I'd prefer the terms 'slight,' or 'petit,' to the current 'puny,' 'half-pint,' 'knee-high'—oh, the hell with it; I'll just march those giants off to Moscow where they'll be out of earshot."
—*William J. O'Connell*
Worcester, Massachusetts

Lord Whipshot sighted along his cruel, aquiline nose to bestow a withering sneer upon the wretched peasant cowering pathetically at his feet, the last wretched pheasant of the season clutched firmly but gently in his mouth; Whipshot's peasants were bred for soft mouths, and a modicum of servility.
—*Jay Cates*
Vancouver, British Columbia, Canada

"An physicke be hir passioun!" ruminated Thump, the burly swain, "sooth will I physicke hir great woundy bodice— nay lave enow thereto those goatsmilk haunches; salve and medicament the livelong day withal yon flaxen-headed wench . . ." and with a parting coarse appeal to the ruder gods, he lurched at last away from the achingly provocative display of Doctor Barbie Fashions behind the mesmerizing, gleaming windows of the Newark Mall.

—*Will Thomson*
Coeur d'Alene, Idaho

Little Dickie wended his way sadly homeward, brushing away a silent tear every time he thought of that note in his pocket from his teacher, which told of how he had been punished for lying about the dog eating his homework; it would break his mother's heart, it would, because dear, good Mrs. Nixon had always taught her Dickie that lying was naughty, very, very naughty.

—*Deborah Berger*
Alexandria, Virginia

As he vengefully pursued the menacing white hulk of the potato around his soup bowl, Captain Ahab thought about how potato cultivation methods symbolized Man versus Nature, the struggle for American independence, his entire life, and Aunt Martha's infidelity; but what he hated most about the potato as he vengefully harpooned it with his prosthetic hook, souvenir of a previous encounter with a spud, was this: it was a vegetable.

—*L. M. Lewis*
Carrollton, Texas

"I always wanted to live in Helena, Montana," he said with a faraway look in his eye; "I'd open a little bistro and call it the 'Handbasket' and the whole world would go there!"
—*Ned Olson*
Kirkland, Washington

"There's a lot more to life than sex, you know!" Bob said enthusiastically upon being introduced to Mrs. Corwell, President of Faux Pas Anonymous.
—*J. J. Solari*
Burbank, California

Jim unzipped his mouth like a gym bag, grinning and gleefully shouting with ecstasy, a course of action that so belied his white lab coat and sterile, test-tube surroundings, because he was sure he had discovered the answer to the nagging question that had plagued men and women regardless of nationality, race, age, or socioeconomic status, and now he actually felt his sweaty palms grasping the Nobel prize for finding just what it is in a dentist's office that triggers the salivary glands to work triple-time-plus-two.
—*Karin Sherbin*
Simsbury, Connecticut

"Rutabaga! Zucchini! Squash!" yelled Norm with all the zeal of a man who, after losing out fourteen times in a row to an old potato farmer named Ed, was determined to win Burt County's fifteenth annual Vegetable Recitation Competition.
—*Peter Nemarich*
New Haven, Connecticut

"Vito and his family had nothing to do with it, Wanda-Sue!" he sighed, twisting his well-worn rhodite Quamsett Valley View High School Class of '58 ring as he gazed intently but not bitterly out of the basement window with his tooled snakeskin boot propped up on the main boiler pressure release valve; "it was fate, and my inborn sense of adventure which led me to sell off the tailor shop in East Jersey and take a job as an industrial refrigerant gauge reader with Ammo-Chill Maintenance here in Tulsa." —*Judith Ann Williams*
Bedford, Texas

Myth: Self-criticism is one of a writer's most important assets.

Reality: Self-criticism will only weaken your self-assurance, the attribute you need more than any other to write. Besides, you will receive enough criticism from those unable to appreciate your work.

Awakening that summer morning in a contemplative, thought-provoking mood, the man, the myth, the legend, Enrico Antonio Julio Gonzales Martinez Smith, the foremost legal mind of our day, could not help but wonder how he, a peasant of Spanish descent, could have been blessed with the looks of Don Juan, oratory skills of Abraham Lincoln, the logic of Socrates, the legal mind of Cardozo, and the personality of a tree slug. —*Timothy G. Orlando*
Warren, Michigan

Joe Malignancy robbed all the jewels and money in Buffy Fiscal's safe, stopped to kick a dog, and started a small brush fire on the way home, but he meant well.

—*Ruth H. Coleman*
Piscataway, New Jersey

George thought how neat it would be to visit the ashram in Kolhapor, to meditate upon the vacuity of western civilization, to apprentice himself to a wise counselor, so that he might devote himself more fully to greater spiritual values, such as the study of Parvati, a well-endowed member of the Hindu celestial pantheon, whose upthrust bare breasts always reminded him of Rhoda, the unpossessed wonder of his tenth-grade homeroom class.

—*Stephen F. Somerstein*
Mountain View, California

Not until the moment of his death would he ever forget the way she stabbed him in the back—but that came a moment later.

—*Craig Oakley*
Berkeley, California

When Samantha Ballandreu walked onstage, she felt not only a thousand eyes eager to watch her as she sang a piece from "The Barber of Seville," but she felt the tender, soft hands of Brad Hopkins, her midget bodyguard whom she hoped was not hiding under her white chiffon evening gown in order to enjoy her bottomless charms, but to engage in his mission of catching the man who had threatened to kill her tonight.

—*Tom Mach*
San Jose, California

As the huge jet began to roar down the runway, Martin closed his eyes and tried to think of something else to take his mind off his fear of flying, but the *whump* of the landing gear being retracted brought him back to the present and the reality that *he* was the pilot of this 747 flying tenement.

—*Liz Forbes*
Warner Robins, Georgia

It was in Pamplona, during the running of the bulls, and I, having recently and mercifully obtained a divorce from the malevolent and threatening Cedric Lytton, was watching a young Spaniard, clad in an imitation suit of lights, leap over a low wall onto the pavement and, without a moment's hesitation, plunge a stout Toledo blade into the throat of the leading bull, causing its immediate demise and prompting me to shout, "Oh, if only the bull were Lytton."

—*Bill Brooks, CAC*
Carmel, Indiana

Humming methodically, Priscilla sat down to pen the tune that would skyrocket her to rock-and-roll superstardom, "Stretch Marks of My Mind." —*Toph Whitmore*
Palo Alto, California

PRINCESS VEGA
BLUSHED A
RADIANT GREEN

Writing science fiction: The real trick to writing science fiction is in making up funny names for aliens. One easy way is to use a Ouija board. You can also find inspiration in the acronyms of government agencies and in radio station call letters.

Princess Vega blushed a radiant green and whispered, "Oh, Captain Brisbane, though you are from Earth, you must not let these superficial differences come between us," then she delicately belched a hair ball into her silk hanky.

—*Mary Lee Ward*
Chicago, Illinois

Commander Brandon surveyed the carnage in the ship—the shattered bodies, bones protruding through lacerated flesh, hair ripped from scalps and plugged into distended jaws, bloood riveleting down consoles and bulkheads, a large chunk of Ensign Dalmar's liver perched atop the astrogation computer—and concluded that it had not been a patricularly good idea to feed a Ceti IV fangworm taco chips.   —*John Floars*
Woodbridge, Virginia

Rocky Balboa, the Italian Stallion, stood before the forbidding black monolith of Europa, tightening the strings on his gloves as he prepared for this, the greatest fight of his career, and remembered the words of his dead trainer Mick—now the luminescent Starchild—who'd come to him in a mystical vision and said to him, making him feel almost God-like: "Something's gonna happen during that last round, Rocky, something wonderful!"   —*Gary A. Braunbeck*
Newark, Ohio

He was born on a small mining asteroid at the edge of the Orion Nebula, unaware of the cataclysmic forces building which would soon plunge humanity into a century of intergalactic war and the universe into primal imbalance; but that is not part of our story.   —*Martin Phinn*
Norwich, Norfolk, England

Worse than the nuclear catastrophe that had killed billions, worse than the fact that the resulting radiation left, despite scientists' prediction, an enlarged species of daisies as the ruling race, worse than all this was that previously innocuous flower's revenge on mankind for years of being downtrodden, which took the form of protracted, and horribly inverted, games of "loves me, loves me not."   —*Janet M. Kaul*
Redwood City, California

Her Majesty's Spaceship *Manly Intent* plunged toward the rogue sun, its huge, throbbing engines thrusting it ever deeper into the chromosphere, but Captain Stonebreaker Smith found his gaze drawn uncontrollably away from the gauges and to the supple, plump, and filmily clad form of Lieutenant (JG) Violet Wildrose, her luscious anatomy oscillating in maddening sympathetic vibrations, igniting a fire in the Stonebreaker's blood hotter than any star, until he could stand it no longer, and, tearing at his spacesuit and lunging across the gravityless cabin, cried, "Ballistics be damned!" as his space-hardened body responded to the task at hand. —*Ray C. Gainey*
Indianapolis, Indiana

Gorvan Yngvie "Babe" Jhoorm XII, Son of Seth, Grand Vizopterix of Irkutsk, Mayor of New Ulan Bator, Fourth Class Adept, Suzeraine (in a previous incarnation) of Exxon, Scourge of the Pleiades, Chancellor of Barnard's Star, slayer of trolls, and the best damn shortstop to ever lay cured ash on a sphere of eohippus hide, woke.   —*Eric Mayer*
Rochester, New York

Simone, diving with the aquatic grace of a barracuda, re-alized only too late that what she assumed was the automatic

pool sweep was actually her mutant half-brother Oscar, the product of a space alien's visitation to her mother, the brother whom she thought she had killed in the sewers of Paris all those years ago.
—*Nancy E. Raff*
San Francisco, California

On revision: There is one final task in editing your novel. Read through it one more time, looking for lost opportunities, for those places where you could have put in more words. Remember, books are for readers, and words are what they read. You are offering your readers a word feast. Let someone else write for verbal dieters. Or, to put the process another way, think of it as plumping up a word pillow.

The alien stared at Captain Veronica Saunders with a warmth not unlike that found on certain of Pluto's outer moons, its black, scaly claws flexing in and out, in and out, its long powerful tail wrapped unmercifully around her curvaceous chest, pinning her arms to her sides, its two-hundred piggy little eyes peering into her very soul with a singularly steady gaze, and it found itself wishing in some dim portion of its tiny brain that this one wouldn't scream so much while being peeled.
—*Jim Menard*
Rochester, New York

"He's dead, Jim," the starship's doctor pronounced solemnly, kneeling over the body, then looking over his shoulder for the captain, "Jim?" he repeated, then, looking down at the body again, said, "Oh, *there* you are, Jim!"

—*John Wenger*
Kalamazoo, Michigan

"WERRY CLEWWER, MR. BLOND!"

On sources: If you want to base a crime or spy story on factual episodes, you are in luck. Government agencies are a veritable treasure trove of information. They keep meticulous records which are open to any curious taxpayer, and government functionaries, especially at the federal level, are delighted to cooperate, even when they or their associates are suspected of laxness or incompetence in the performance of their duties. If you want to base a novel on the Walker spy case, for example, your only problem will be in sorting through the tons of material you can expect from eager-to-please civil servants. Remember, the authorities just love to demonstrate that they are just that—*authorities*, people with more plentiful and accurate information than anyone else.

"Werry clewwer, Mr. Blond, but no clewwer enough," lisped Elmer as he slowly levered his shotgun at the now somewhat alarmed British secret service agent peering out of a bright yellow rabbit suit.
—*Jaan Pesti*
Wilmington, Delaware

The lily-livered NATO traitor, Reginal Crawley, and his ruthless, calculating, communist counterpart, Werner Schnitzel, whispered under the shadowed archway of the Franz Josef I Memorial by the Albertinaplatz, as the steely gray light of coming dawn spread across the eastern Vienna sky, and as CIA Special Agent Derrick "Meatloaf" Hammond, hiding behind a nearby column, strained to hear them over the moan of pent wind, cursing his last night's meal of beans on toast.
—*Peter L. Stafford*
Los Gatos, California

Blair Corp, ace spy, didn't appreciate Headquarters' humor when, squeezing the hair trigger of the perfectly balanced, titanium-framed, no-glare-black-anodized centennial edition Fenninger automatic, the hairy-knuckled henchmen of Titus Manacle found, not a salvo of 9 mm. slugs tearing through their scouring-pad chests, but, instead, gooblets of anchovy paste besplattering their Hawaiian shirts.
—*Raphael X. Reichert*
Fresno, California

With the last sutures in place, an exultant sigh of relief mingled with ecstasy escaped the lips of the renowned plastic surgeon, Dr. William Howard Chesterton III of Boston, grateful that at last those long years of training and living the Lie had finally paid off—for no one even suspected that his real

identity was Sergei Potemkin Vladivostak and that he had just succeeded in implanting a Soviet listening device during the breast enlargement surgery of America's First Lady.
—*Nancy O'Denius*
St. Louis, Missouri

A strapping bull of a man with bloodshot eyes like the arteries of the Los Angeles freeway system, the outline of a .357 Magnum showing through his yellow-and-black-striped, torso-tight designer bowling shirt, he stood in the middle of the Palazzo San Marco sucking on a capriciously dripping raspberry Popsicle, and as I peered through my binoculars from atop the narrow walkway which surrounded the hallowed cupola of the cathedral, I knew, as if by some mysterious, centuries-old mystic intuition, that here at last, vulnerable as a Rolls-Royce on a San Jose drag strip, was Interpol's most wanted terrorist.
—*Peter Fleming, S.J.*
San Francisco, California

The moonlight reflected on midnight's snowfall, as Padrick hitched up his double truss and winked slyly at Sister Moose McGuire, who gave her habit a final tug before removing the parachute harness and donning the radio headset, readying herself for the transmission of their position behind Soviet lines in search of the missing Watergate tapes.
—*Dave Williams*
Campbell, California

Derek came to, his gun-shot bicep throbbing, each pulse telegraphing his brain in the macabre, hematoid Morse code of the martially mutilated, and reaching to massage his numbed thighs, he discovered with explosive annoyance that they—

not unlike his coolly effective Beretta automatic and silencer—
were gone, yet the riveting image of the First Lady being
ravaged by the swarthy Russian croquet team triaged self-
examination, wrenching him upright onto his tanned and heavily muscled stumps—which he wryly observed to be uneven.
                                    —*Peter van Rijsbergen*
                                    Novato, California

It was a sticky situation, and Percival, as he wiped the
glutinous glob of Scottish porridge off the lapel of his second-
best Harris tweed jacket—and his best Harris ripped only the
previous fortnight when he crawled through the barbed wire—
then carefully peeled his boiled egg (for this was Sunday breakfast time) pondered that, as surely as the porridge spitball had
been aimed accurately in his direction, his cover was most
assuredly blown.
                                    —*Patricia J. Andeweg*
                                    Dallas, Texas

Walking inconspicuously along a grimy East Berlin side street
that cold and overcast November morning, Hans von Roloff,
the spy without a conscience, realized he had put on the wrong
trench coat that morning and, instead of the canister of mi-
crofilm he sought, fished out of his pocket the unfinished and
slightly moldy portion of sauerbraten (hold the kraut) he had
bought last week from a vender on the Unter den Linden.
                                    —*Jon Krampner*
                                    Los Angeles, California

Steely eyes narrowing, Dirk Bork elevated one of his equally
dexterous hands to reveal the presence of his customized
Arrghoffle Mark IV .99 caliber repeating shot pistol (the now-
dead blind gunsmith's greatest achievement), expertly fired a

single shot through the window which split the aorta of the Ninja assassin (who, disciplined unto death, fell silently down the rugged cliff face, his garb, black as the floor of a Texaco, disappearing into the night), and then resumed his coitus with the Countess Felicia von Schanzmann, heir to her family's licorice fortune and the woman who just might be holding the fate of the free world in the palm of the hand that wasn't busy.

—*Tim Marlowe*
Arcadia, California

As the Gestapo agent's screams reached a hideous crescendo of agonized wailing, the *Maquis* operative shut off his flame-thrower, dragged the crocodiles away, disconnected the electrodes, beat off the swarms of maddened hornets, and, removing the whimpering Nazi from the vat of boiling sulfuric acid, turned to Thrummedstopple and said, "Well, *mon ami*, you were right, he couldn't take it!"

—*Robert D. Norris, Jr.*
Tulsa, Oklahoma

IN DUBIOUS TASTE

Explicit and implicit narration: Some things need to be spelled out for your readers, some not:

"Looking back and forth expectantly from her to the bed, he put his hands together and made a diving motion."

This *shows* rather than *tells* that the character is ready for S-E-X. More seasoned readers will appreciate this subtlety.

"Cha, cha, cha!" I whispered merrily in Mary Ellen's ear, as I escorted her stiff and lifeless body around the dance floor, proud of the envy I aroused in the fellows who had always dreamed of being this close to the once vibrant cheerleader, but more than a little ashamed of the means I had to use to get this date.
—*Richard Hemphill*
Montreal, Quebec, Canada

"Tomorrow," moaned Esmeralda as she clutched the supine form of her sleeping lover more firmly to her heaving bosom, "to—nay, *tonight*"—she tensed as her waters broke and flooded the love-stained sheets—"I will tell Lord Rampart that I bear his child!"
—*Lisa J. Evans*
Malden, Massachusetts

The moon was dark, dark and bright, while the sun was hot and very high up in the sky when Jennifer finally broke down and wept very bitterly, her shoulders heaving like the burping lid of a pot of popcorn and her nasal passages making those pathetic, snot-choked, sucking sounds that the truly sad are wont to make.
—*Janice Lee*
Edmonton, Alberta, Canada

As she shaved her legs, Bambi gasped with masochistic pleasure at the bloody strips of flesh that flew from her Lady Shick like curls of mahogany from a carpenter's plane.
—*Wendy Gergick*
Rose Mary Gergick
Tonganoxie, Kansas

"Catarrh! Diarrhea! Phthisis!" rang out the merry cry of the disease peddler as he dragged his reeking cart through the

festering alleys of London, tossing samples to the jolly, shouting crowd of urchins, waifs, and toddlers that surrounded him, and he continued, "Hemorrhoids! Gonorrhea! Encephalitis! Yaws! Pox! Croup! Ha, ha, ha! Who'll pay a tuppenny fer one o' me bonny plagues?"
—*Brian W. Holmes*
San Jose, California

Six of one or half-a-dozen of another, that's what we forensic proctologists have to put up with every day of our professional lives!
—*W. R. C. Shedenhelm*
Ventura, California

I have never enjoyed a rude shock, so it was with much consternation that, on the evening of July tenth, I should come across the severed toes of the school librarian in the pocket of my green windbreaker.
—*John Geoffrey Alnutt*
Brooklyn, New York

Shannon's love for her cello was obvious to everyone in the concert hall, though few imagined that this love extended beyond pure musical lyricism and had taken on a raw physicality in which the instrument's deep reverberations shot through the cellulite of her outstretched thighs, fulfilling her in a way Bach alone never could.
—*Craig Sweat*
Atlanta, Georgia

As the wind whipped Audry's vomit against the vibrant yellow Porsche, and her stomach geared up for the next onslaught of G forces, she realized she had, yet again, been conned into another Sunday drive with Jack, but perusing the sun glistening off the crusting remains of her tomato soup and corn tamales, she smiled inwardly, knowing she had extracted her subtle revenge.

(from *Queasy on the Curves*)   —*Diane Lynne Pierce*
                                                                Martinez, California

Lord Cecil leaned over the balustrade and surveyed the gowned and uniformed dancers whirling and writhing across the ebony-and-crimson-checkered ballroom floor, then drew deeply on his Cuban-Corona Maxima-extra cigar, and disdainfully flicked a drooping ash toward the floor, and watched it drift downward until it came to rest in Lady Beverly's décolletage, where it remained unnoticed until later in the evening when her lover, Baron Rodney, licked it from her skin while trying to lift the Hope diamond from about her crepey throat.   —*Earl Sullaway*
                                                                Sacramento, California

The air made a sound like a castanet player on amphetamines as it rattled through the old man's wasted lungs for the last time, and it made him think suddenly of Tijuana, old Andre Kostelanetz records, and all the margaritas he had peed away; and what the hell had ever happened to mustachioed Maria and her grizzled burro named Phil?
                                                                —*Kathy Ellington*
                                                                Oakland, California

Clad only in the skimpy gold lamé apron that she often donned to inspire herself through afternoons committed to baking for local charities, Irene began to tire of her between-bath ritual of alternately exposing her buttocks to a sun lamp

and performing excruciating sets of fanny-firming squat thrusts, and she sighed impatiently as she waited for her buns to rise and brown.
—*Sibyl Darter*
Granada Hills, California

A pitcher of lemonade later, plodding along behind the roaring lawn mower, Mickey realized there was one sure way to see whether electricity could travel upstream.
—*James Russell Davis*
Sunnyvale, California

Reginald was a little surprised at Lady Gwendolyn's exuberance on their wedding night, but not nearly as surprised as he was when he discovered that the two white bands he had mistaken for sexy stocking-garters encircling Lady Gwendolyn's delicate thighs were, in fact, a pair of Hartz Flea and Tick Collars.
—*L. W. Thomas*
Oxford, Mississippi

On morality in fiction: Moral victories are fine for moralists; your readers want physical ones.

The staccato of appreciation for Emily's bean dip, echoing off the seats of the Chippendales and wafting toward the rococo ceiling, was surpassed only by the guests' glee over the availability of lamb-chop panties with which to daintily wipe besmirched mouths.

—Nancy Wambach
Hollis Logue
San Jose, California

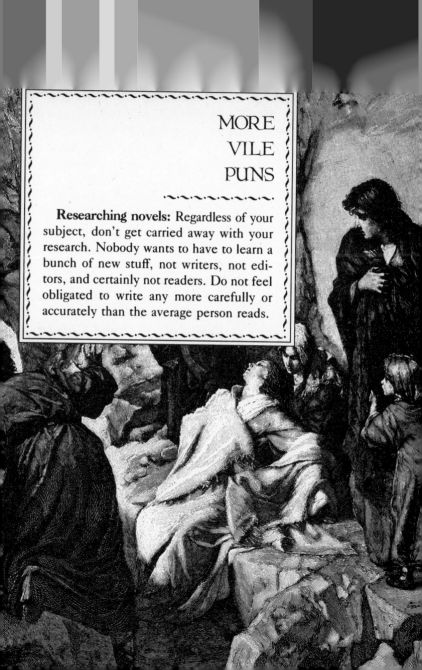

MORE
VILE
PUNS

Researching novels: Regardless of your subject, don't get carried away with your research. Nobody wants to have to learn a bunch of new stuff, not writers, not editors, and certainly not readers. Do not feel obligated to write any more carefully or accurately than the average person reads.

"Caramba! Madre de Dios!" shouted Capitan Don Lardo. "I try to order some fettucine from Luigi's in Vera Cruz, and this accursed idiot of an orderly brings me the head of Alfredo Garcia!"
—*Robert D. Norris, Jr.*
Tulsa, Oklahoma

Looking down from the camp's vantage point atop the Tehachapi Mountains the morning after breaking his holy vows by slipping away to be with the beautiful Serrano maiden, on the fact that the earth *really did* move unnoticed in their passion, the humble explorer (and later to be canonized) Padre Andreas looked, stunned, at the wreckage and destruction spread out up and down the length of Alta California, and said to himself, "This cannot be *my* fault, can it?"
—*Gordon K. Anderson*
Jeffrey C. Sadler
Crestline, California

Trussed to the masthead like a fatted goose, Drusilla writhed futilely against her Viking captor's ungodly lust, trying desperately to cast herself into the frigid sea—only to be reined (alas, again) by his piston arms as he roared, "You vill remain in da boat; the Sven is mightier than the fjord!"
—*Carrie Sogg*
San Francisco, California

Reclining by the banks of Cleveland's majestic Cuyahoga, the poet and exiled pretender Nicolae Krepuskula sucked from his feathery moustache a final soupçon of peppery headcheese and envisioned with trenchant nostalgia his Moldavian homeland, where he, an orphan playing near the mighty Dniester, would raise his only toy, an encrusted plumber's helper, and

thrusting it like a bejeweled scepter toward the final throne of his father, would cry out, "Oh, Beloved Sire! Kick the slats from your bare box and dream along with me; I'm on my way to the tsars!" —*William Overstreet*
Pittsburgh, Pennsylvania

Azure du Smelbad de Islamamamabaad climbed down from the elephant, steadied his legs from the long, queasy ride across the Himalayas, turned green as he looked at his mahout, and said, "Ah'm Sikh!" —*Michael L. Chadwell*
Duluth, Georgia

As the sultry southern son set his banjo on the porch, he pondered pensively on his Spanish Catholic parents, the poor but honest Juan and Oblivia, and on his grandfather, whose garbled wise old sayings resulted in Grandpa being unkindly referred to as the village idiom, and on Zebediah Slumlord, owner of Miserable Mountain (a hideous appelation) on which they barely lived, and on Zeb's daughter, Sleazy Belle, of whose slightly crossed eye the banjo-plucking Juan Boy was the apple, and on Emmy Sally Jo Bergerstein, the Jewish girl from Richmond, whom the Catholic Juan Boy planned to marry, in which case he would seek from Father Christian White, the parish priest, a mixed blessing.

—*Anna Jean Mayhew*
Chapel Hill, North Carolina

Vaulting over the wall and scurrying down the bank, the internationally hunted dwarf spy Jan Pryvicalya scurried through Prague's cobblestoned streets, deposited the envelope addressed to Edward Teller in the customary safe place, then— much to his credit—slithered through the overdraft of the

American Embassy and, having regained his balance, breath-lessly whispered to the nonplussed duty officer, "Can you cache a small Czech?"
—*John Israel*
Charlottesville, Virginia

It was a drizzling cold dawn in the late spring of 1887 in the great stone courtyard of the garrison headquarters of the Prochazka Guards in Prague as Lieutenant Anton Bedrich Hlavacek, wastrel, cheater at cards, and all-around cad, was led out of the barracks to the roll of drums and the scorn of his fellow soldiers to be stripped in rank in that most rare and dramatic of all military ceremonies in the Austro-Hungarian Empire—cashiering a bad Czech.
—*Katherine B. Rambo*
Foster City, California

"Undulate!" he commanded, and began to play, as the cobra in the wicker basket cunningly unwound herself and spread her hood in preparation for the finale to a career she had never sought, reflecting venomously that in only moments she would be leaving this charmed life behind to strike out on her own.
—*Jennifer R. Sanders*
Houston, Texas

Watteau, all six hundred pounds of him, had been a master truffle rooter for years, and Jean-Luc couldn't bear to eat him but, on the other hand, couldn't bear his swinish noises and, so, paid dearly to have the old boar's larynx removed, which, perhaps, explains why, seemingly content in the rich Bourgogne mud, Watteau was, in fact, disgruntled.
—*Raphael X. Reichert*
Fresno, California

Our story opens with our gallant heroes, the dashing Monterey Jack; his true love, the beauteous yet sprightly Fontina, and their faithful yet comical companions, maladroit Gouda and impetuous Feta, intrepid secret agents for the mysterious, albeit saintly Gruyère, head of the Fromage resistance and sworn nemesis of the wicked, debauched, yet sensitive Count Emmentaler, who seeks Gruyère's true identity, having rescued Fontina's father, the brilliant Dr. Emiliano Parmesan, from the malevolent, power-mad, albeit pensive Count's ruinous, even drafty castle of Neufchâtel, furnished in more than Oriental splendor on a crag above Port du Salut, and escaped to Paris where we find them one week later on the Pont l'Évêque, perturbed as they are suddenly confronted by a fearsome, semi-solid, moldy blue blob bubbling noxiously above the panic-stricken roofs of the Rue de Camembert—the hideous, even loathsome Gorgonzola, vile unsavory pet of the fiendishly clever, even, as our agitated heroes realize in horror, playful Count who appears, demanding with a diabolical smirk, "Take me to your Liederkranz!"

—Katherine B. Rambo
Foster City, California

Launcelot lay upon the bed, exhausted, as his partner, the smiling Guinevere, remarked, "That's what I call a knight well-spent."
—Michael McGarel
Park Forest, Illinois

Sitting in the German barroom, Lennie begged, "Plee-ze, George, please—lemme have just one more chocolate mouse!" but even as he spoke he sensed the futility of this request, kind of idiomatically knowing that George had seen him previously, secretly dipping another rodent in his beer in the rear of the hall by the john, in a stein beck there.

—*Tom Harmon*
Manassas, Virginia

Tex Hooter dug the worn heels of his boots more firmly into the manure-fragrant ground, glared at the young cowpoke with his one good eye, and snarled, "Why, yuh varmint! Ah may be gittin' too old to rope an' too shaky to shoot an' too toothless to spit, but Ah still knows the subjunctive mood when Ah sees it, and yuh got tuh say, 'Ah believe them cows 'ud be a sight happier in the corral if the *bull were lit in.*' "

—*Nancy Wambach*
San Jose, California

On dialogue: Dialogue is more than mere words. It is timing. Sometimes, depending on how you feel, your characters will trade snappy quips, staccato fashion. Other times, the pace will slacken:

"Have a cup of tea?" I asked her.

She demurred four minutes, then replied, "I'll have two."

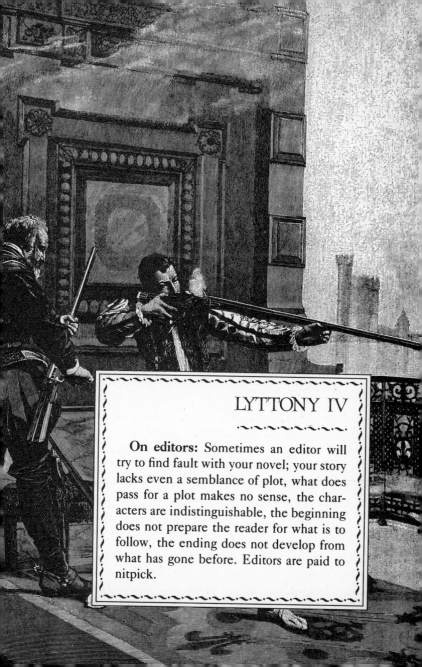

LYTTONY IV

On editors: Sometimes an editor will try to find fault with your novel; your story lacks even a semblance of plot, what does pass for a plot makes no sense, the characters are indistinguishable, the beginning does not prepare the reader for what is to follow, the ending does not develop from what has gone before. Editors are paid to nitpick.

"I knew it! I knew it!" Edmond exclaimed as the ship sailed over the edge.
—*Mary V. Brown*
Ventura, California

Reading was something Jay knew about only from books, yet he was quite anxious to experience it for himself.

—*Stephen D. Bock*
Marietta, Georgia

Pat dreamily fingered the large "W" imprint that Richard's Whittier College sweater had left on her bare abdomen; this and their other night of passion would produce the loveliest pair of daughters she could have ever imagined (though Julie, poor thing, inherited Richard's massive, flapping jowls).
—*Christopher Kochmanski*
Ypsilanti, Michigan

When I first met Hedy, she was that rare kind of girl-woman who could successfully carry off a punk-rock, Day-Glo hairdo while wearing a thousand-dollar Dior and playing Chopin on a concert grand while keeping time with tiny feet clad in scuffed Adidas.
—*Bart Kull*
Alexandria, Virginia

Life fairly reeked with joy for Pietro and his fellow immigrants once they had settled in America, although they often felt far removed from their European homelands, thanks mostly to the Atlantic Ocean.
—*Hawk*
Gainesville, Florida

THE LITERARY MEMOIR

As a young girl living in Paris, I wore a white hat, a peculiar hat that resides vividly in my memory, so vividly that to this day I can describe it in exquisite, uncompromising detail, and it is not so much the hat, of course, but that compulsion to describe it which should suggest, to any but the most indifferent of intellects, an almost supernatural sensitivity, an incredible refinement which you are free to marvel at— as I confess I do myself—and now, remembering that hat, whose whiteness was like perfume . . .

—*William Browning Spencer*
Vienna, California

"You speak truly when you say that only the lead elephant was struck and killed by your train," said mahout Paramjit Rajeshwar Singh to the driver of the Calcutta to Hyderabad Express following the accident at the level crossing, then his eyes filled with tears as he asked, "but of what use are the remaining pachyderms, nine of whom have had their tails ripped out?" —*Ron Leeming*
Edmonton, Alberta, Canada

"It would have been better indeed to have saved one of them for tomorrow's Long Pig Casserole," thought Ouga-Ouga, the cannibal chef, and he watched pensively as Jacques Pate, *le maître* of Chez Fromage, his sous-chef, Andres, and the patissiere, Louis, simmered slowly in the island version of a

crockpot coconut-consommé; "For it is truly written that too many cooks spoil the broth."
—*T. O'Carroll*
San Jose, California

Transported from 1987 Mill Valley to 399 B.C. Athens by his fiery time machine—a nuclear-powered, turbo-charged BMV—Randy Esterhaus recalled all his intensive est classes, standing on the steps of the Parthenon, confronting the Grecian gadfly, and gushing like a chilly cheerleader at homecoming, "But look on the bright side—that vial of hemlock you have at home is not half-empty, it's half-full!"
—*Tom Suddick*
San Jose, California

My story begins in the womb where I was really getting bored of a steady diet of amniotic fluid, experiencing constant motion sickness, and my mother never letting me go anywhere.
—*Connie Fox*
Thorne Bay, Alaska

It was not just the whiplike *whup* sound under the hood of the little red, white, and blue Datsun truck—you know, like the sound squirrels make when they are shot off rocks—which alerted Bill and Frank of their impending peril on Interstate 84, fifteen miles from Mountain Home, that windy night when the highway glowed like a gross gray snake and the horizon hovered gloomily like, unbeknown to them, the evil lurking in the truck's water pump; no, it was not just that, for there were many things, not the least of which was their shared knowledge that in five hours they would be in Pocatello.
—*Frank L. Lundburg*
Boise, Idaho

Martha's thighs were sheathed in "Despair," a designer hose of the fishnet variety, the type that allowed the tightly bound patches of cellulite to rub together as she bounded across the bare boards, deliberate in her attempts to provoke a reaction from Sidney, the half-witted hunchback who lived directly below—if you could call boiling camel heads for the local natural history museum all day a living.

—*John Waid*
Newtownabbey, Northern Ireland

Count Pierre Dmitri Alyosha (or Misha to his friends) Badsky slapped his rival Prince Ivanovich Pytor (his saint's name) Gregorovich Rasputinovich's evil, sneering, callous, pockmarked, twisted face with a sour cream-and-caviar-filled blin sauteed in vodka, for he—Prince Ivanovich, that is—had impaled and impregnated the honor, chastity, and virginity of his fiancée—of Misha's fiancée, that is—the ravishingly, stunningly, hauntingly beautiful Anna Natasha Olga Fedorovna, whose limpid, liquid Bambi fawn eyes and delicate narrow head and slender neck reminded the Prince of his elegant Russian wolfhound, Spotsky. —*Wilda Waldo Williams*
New York, New York

"Jiminy Crickets!" exclaimed Corporal Ashley Jones at the control panel of Nuclear Response Silo #36 in the Black Hills of South Dakota, "I guess I must've pushed the wrong button . . ." —*Joe Ecclesine*
San Diego, California

As I look back over all the loves in my life, none was so overpowering as that of Clark, the boy in my seventh-grade English class, whose eyes were as green as the swimming pool

my mother had installed the summer before she was put in the wheelchair, and was thus too preoccupied to concern herself with its general maintenance. —*Theresa Ambrose*
Holliston, Massachusetts

"It *was* a shark!" Anne Thormby-Knight hooted with lusty gusto as she pulled her arm out of the water and triumphantly wagged her bloody stump at the doubters in the dinghy.
—*Daniel Orozco*
San Francisco, California

As the giant mole rat cried, "Toady!," gave a keening death rattle, and lurched against the history-encrusted walls of the quasi-neo-Edwardian burrow, Archibald MacEliowhee, the hirsute (some might say) *éminence gris* of the Hollywood directing community, realized that his horror remake of Kenneth Grahame's *The Wind in the Willows* was wounded beyond redemption ten million dollars and ten months into production, and he retched so violently that he brought up the autographed copy of *Das Kapital* with embroidered bookplates that he had swallowed in a moment of panic during the Eisenhower administration. —*Peter B. Williams*
Vancouver, British Columbia, Canada

It was a dark and stormy night when it happened as I had seen it happen a thousand times in my mind's eye: he dragged his misshapen form slowly toward me, paused, spat the bloody product of a racking, ominous cough onto the sidewalk, wiped the red-flecked spittle from his greasy lips with the ragged sleeve of a filthy raincoat, and, in the dim yellow porch light, grinned hideously up at me with broken, yellow teeth, speak-

ing the words I had been dreading for sixteen years, "Hi, Miz Johnson, I'm Billy, and I'm here to take Cindy to the prom!"
—*John Norton*
Charlottesville, Virginia

On revision: Think of cutting a story and boning chicken breasts. After you finish pulling and prying and tearing the meat away from the bones, you have a pile of leftover scraps ideal for stir-frying. These are the elements of your writing that you can use to cook up your next story. Discard nothing.

"What we have in common, Jerry," the hooker told the evangelist on our global telethon, while cash registers rang furiously in the background, "is that we're both against free love."
—*Kenneth Schulze*
Rocky River, Ohio

LITTLE
DID I KNOW

On endings: In the last chapter all conflicts should be resolved, all questions answered, and all issues cleared up:

"Then you mean . . . ?"

"Yes, darling, it was all a big misunderstanding. No one was hurt, nothing really went wrong, everyone is satisfied, and there is nothing left to do."

Little did I know when I accepted the offer of Sir Hugo de Grave, saturnine master of Malvue Manor, to be governess to his ward Miss Charity, that I would be embarking on a series of adventures which would include ghostly visitations in the chapel, a narrow escape from death at the hands of the Specter of the Crypt, undreamed-of ecstasy in the arms of Sir Hugo, and the triumph of overcoming Miss Charity's tendency to split infinitives.   —*Lucy Shores*
                                 Hartford, Connecticut

If Melvin Fitcarmody hadn't been washed ashore in Antibes; if Katia Dhargomiszky hadn't broken her pinkie the night before the Rose Bowl Game; if Roger Washington hadn't seen fit to alter the Murgatroyd's Abyssinian cat—a mangy, ill-tempered brute named Pregnant Paws—but that's another story, and as I sit here nursing the mother and father of all hangovers, I often wonder if Bill Burgison would still be alive if Maggy Armstrong hadn't said yes to Storm Stream instead of me.   —*Julia Buonocore*
                                    New York, New York

If I had not slipped that day in a puddle of cat vomit and slid into the arms of Jason, the building contractor, thus triggering a sneezing fit because of my allergies which responded to the coating of dry-wall dust on his blue denim leisure suit, my life might have been quite different.
                       —*Christine Freeman*
                       Vancouver, British Columbia, Canada

As the terrorists detonated the one-megaton nuclear bomb they had planted atop the Empire State Building, thousands of miles away, in the Tibetan highlands of China, in his little

village of Hau-bu-hau-chr, unconcerned and unaffected by the politics of his own or of any other country, Bok-choy, the left-handed weaver whose mother had died when he was three and who was therefore raised with the help of his aunt, worked quickly but carefully, in the way that he had learned from his family as far back as anyone in Hau-bu-hau-chr could remember, making the wide-rimmed, three-handled basket, which he wished above all else to display before all his fellow villagers at the next full moon, hoping that he would thereby finally get the attention of that young maiden with the long, rose-petal-strewn hair whom he had first seen at the laundry pond hunting a titwillow bird with a broken wing which made him a hard hunter to run from.   —*Craig Oakley*
Berkeley, California

How could Octar have known—after years of travail, suffering, hardship, and deprivation; after the exhilaration of Windsor Castle and the degradation of the Black Hole; after leaving a trail of shrunken pocketbooks and swollen wombs all through Asia, the Middle East, and the Peloponnesos—how could he have known he would end up on the dusty, dry, desolate, depleted, demoralizing Arizona reservation, imparting to the Apaches all he knew about the ancient rite of circumcision, and being adored and revered by the natives who lovingly called him the Moyel of the Mescaleros?
—*Howard Kornblum*
Philadelphia, Pennsylvania

Once upon a time, in a land parched by a merciless sun, where grizzled, iron-tough cattlemen waged constant warfare against the elements, Indians, rustlers, taxes, and the local Mafia gunmen from gray slums of Chicago, overseen by god-

father Don Ragonni, and where Louis, the postal pilot android, had become enamored of Clementine, the blue-eyed lass who worked as grease monkey in her father's uptown galaxy interspace vehicle service station, to whom Louis often quoted sonnets by Donne and Wordsworth, and where hard-core detectives roamed sunny streets of the West Coast in search of illegal substances being smuggled into the region by various degenerate characters disguised as Hare Krishna fanatics, there was this guy.
—*Mindi S. Woolman*
Indianapolis, Indiana

She didn't realize, as she drove home from her dentist's office that, precisely as she crossed over into the middle lane, she placed herself directly behind the '81 Chevy carrying the man who would one day marry her, and on another, undo all the dental work she'd ever had before he beat her to death with the sash weight that now rested in his trunk on a copy of the October 9, 1976, edition of the *Bismuth Falls Clarion* which carried his picture on the front page at his Eagle Scout Court of Honor.
—*Kristen Kingsburg Henshaw*
Wakefield, Massachusetts

As he hid from the zombis, who were nattily dressed in the flamboyant and waterproof Hawaiian shirts they had taken from the Libyan terrorists, and watched the extraterrestrials attack the city, as had been predicted by a certain weekly newspaper, Dexter clutched anxiously the tin of smoked salmon-flavored jelly-beans, his favorite, taken from a Chinese deli under the very noses of the Kiwanis Club, which met there every Wednesday and often ordered the spiced rice cakes, despite the Surgeon General's warning, and, reminded of the military action in which he had taken part years ago, thought this an odd way to celebrate his birthday.

—*Leigh Moore*
Denmark, Wisconsin

I was set upon by a roving band of Spanish winos who kidnapped me and forced me to flamenco-dance naked in the display window of an orthopedic shoe salon, until, when I crumpled exhausted and unconscious, they hurled me over the falls, from the maelstrom of which I was pulled to shore by an eccentric retired cartographer who held me captive in his basement (where he was drawing a full-scale map of Lackawanna), forcing me to sharpen pencils relentlessly, my only sustenance the few crumbs that trailed his art gum eraser and a chocolate eclair I thoughtfully had secreted in my beaded handbag.

(from *Debbie Does Niagara*)

—*Richard P. Walters*
Boulder, Colorado

As he crouched, rubbing Lemon Pledge into the already lustrous finish of his Beeman-Webley Air Rifle, Vernon couldn't help but contemplate the cruel hand that an unfeeling world had dealt him; if only the American people had not replaced lovable, bumbling Gerry Ford with the wimpy Jimmy Carter, if only Jimmy Carter had not abandoned the shah of Iran, if only the Ayatollah Khomeini had not canceled all existing Iranian arms contracts (including everything from F-15 fighters to air rifles for training), then he never could have gotten such a good deal on his gun, and he never could have accidentally shot Mrs. Drew's favorite dog and set in motion that turn of events that had led inexorably to the present situation of his being forced to try to save Zomba, the tentacled Betelgeusian, their love-child Horace, and the entire universe (of course!) from the evil hordes of that mad Syrian (from the Dog Star, not the rather nasty little country north of Israel), Emperor Fluffy, with nothing but a stupid BB gun.

—*Thomas Edward Phillips, Jr.*
Naperville, Illinois

On getting a name: In writing, as in everything else, the rich only get richer. Hence, it is easier to get your stuff published after you are a famous author. Thus, make your first publication effort an easy one. Do a book on advice for writers.

ENTER THE BULWER-LYTTON
FICTION CONTEST

The Bulwer-Lytton Fiction Contest is an annual event that asks entrants to compose the worst possible opening sentence to a novel. Anyone anywhere may enter. The rules are simple:

1) Sentences may be of any length and entrants may submit more than one, but all entries must be original and previously unpublished.
2) Entries will be judged by categories, from "general" to detective, western, science fiction, romance, and so on. There will be overall winners as well as category winners.
3) Entries should be submitted on index cards, the sentence on one side and the entrant's name, address, and phone number on the other.
4) The deadline is April 15 (chosen because Americans associate it with another painful submission).

Send your entries to: Bulwer-Lytton Fiction Contest
Department of English
San Jose State University
San Jose, CA 95192-0090